Mental Health Law
in Nursing

Transforming Nursing Practice series

Transforming Nursing Practice is the first series of books designed to help students meet the requirements of the NMC Standards and Essential Skills Clusters for degree programmes. Each book addresses a core topic, and together they cover the generic knowledge required for all fields of practice.

Core knowledge titles:
Series editor: Professor Shirley Bach, Head of the School of Nursing and Midwifery at the University of Brighton

Acute and Critical Care in Adult Nursing	ISBN 978 0 85725 842 7
Becoming a Registered Nurse: Making the Transition to Practice	ISBN 978 0 85725 931 8
Communication and Interpersonal Skills in Nursing (2nd edn)	ISBN 978 0 85725 449 8
Contexts of Contemporary Nursing (2nd edn)	ISBN 978 1 84445 374 0
Dementia Care in Nursing	ISBN 978 0 85725 873 1
Getting into Nursing	ISBN 978 0 85725 895 3
Health Promotion and Public Health for Nursing Students	ISBN 978 0 85725 437 5
Introduction to Medicines Management in Nursing	ISBN 978 1 84445 845 5
Law and Professional Issues in Nursing (2nd edn)	ISBN 978 1 84445 372 6
Leadership, Management and Team Working in Nursing	ISBN 978 0 85725 453 5
Learning Skills for Nursing Students	ISBN 978 1 84445 376 4
Medicines Management in Adult Nursing	ISBN 978 1 84445 842 4
Medicines Management in Children's Nursing	ISBN 978 1 84445 470 9
Medicines Management in Mental Health Nursing	ISBN 978 0 85725 049 0
Nursing Adults with Long Term Conditions	ISBN 978 0 85725 441 2
Nursing and Collaborative Practice (2nd edn)	ISBN 978 1 84445 373 3
Nursing and Mental Health Care	ISBN 978 1 84445 467 9
Passing Calculations Tests for Nursing Students (2nd edn)	ISBN 978 1 44625 642 8
Patient and Carer Participation in Nursing	ISBN 978 0 85725 307 1
Patient Assessment and Care Planning in Nursing	ISBN 978 0 85725 858 8
Patient Safety and Managing Risk in Nursing	ISBN 978 1 44626 688 5
Psychology and Sociology in Nursing	ISBN 978 0 85725 836 6
Safeguarding Adults in Nursing Practice	ISBN 978 1 44625 638 1
Successful Practice Learning for Nursing Students (2nd edn)	ISBN 978 0 85725 315 6
Using Health Policy in Nursing	ISBN 978 1 44625 646 6
What is Nursing? Exploring Theory and Practice (3rd edn)	ISBN 978 0 85725 975 2

Personal and professional learning skills titles:
Series editors: Dr Mooi Standing, Independent Academic Consultant (UK and International) & Accredited NMC Reviewer and Professor Shirley Bach, Head of the School of Nursing and Midwifery at the University of Brighton

Clinical Judgement and Decision Making in Nursing	ISBN 978 1 84445 468 6
Critical Thinking and Writing for Nursing Students (2nd edn)	ISBN 978 1 44625 644 2
Evidence-based Practice in Nursing (2nd edn)	ISBN 978 1 44627 090 5
Information Skills for Nursing Students	ISBN 978 1 84445 381 8
Reflective Practice in Nursing (2nd edn)	ISBN 978 1 44627 085 1
Succeeding in Essays, Exams & OSCEs for Nursing Students	ISBN 978 0 85725 827 4
Succeeding in Research Project Plans and Literature Reviews for Nursing Students	ISBN 978 0 85725 264 7
Successful Professional Portfolios for Nursing Students	ISBN 978 0 85725 457 3
Understanding Research for Nursing Students (2nd edn)	ISBN 978 1 44626 761 5

Mental health nursing titles:
Series editors: Sandra Walker, Senior Teaching Fellow in Mental Health in the Faculty of Health Sciences, University of Southampton and Professor Shirley Bach, Head of the School of Nursing and Midwifery at the University of Brighton

Assessment and Decision Making in Mental Health Nursing	ISBN 978 1 44626 820 9
Mental Health Law in Nursing	ISBN 978 0 85725 761 1

You can find more information on each of these titles and our other learning resources at www.sagepub. co.uk. Many of these titles are also available in various e-book formats, please visit our website for more information.

Mental Health Law in Nursing

Richard Murphy and Philip Wales

Los Angeles | London | New Delhi
Singapore | Washington DC

Learning Matters
An imprint of SAGE Publications Ltd
1 Oliver's Yard
55 City Road
London EC1Y 1SP

SAGE Publications Inc.
2455 Teller Road
Thousand Oaks, California 91320

SAGE Publications India Pvt Ltd
B 1/I 1 Mohan Cooperative Industrial Area
Mathura Road
New Delhi 110 044

SAGE Publications Asia-Pacific Pte Ltd
3 Church Street
#10-04 Samsung Hub
Singapore 049483

Editor: Alex Clabburn
Development editor: Caroline Sheldrick
Production controller: Chris Marke
Project management: Swales & Willis Ltd, Exeter, Devon
Marketing manager: Tamara Navaratnam
Cover design: Wendy Scott
Typeset by: C&M Digitals (P) Ltd, Chennai, India
Printed by: Henry Ling Limited at The Dorset Press, Dorchester, DT1 1HD

Library of Congress Control Number: 2013947938

British Library Cataloguing in Publication data

A catalogue record for this book is available from the British Library

ISBN 978-0-8572-5863-2
ISBN 978-0-8572-5761-1 (pbk)

Contents

About the authors

Richard Murphy is a qualified social worker and still practises as an AMHP and DOLS best interest assessor. He became the Mental Health Act and Mental Capacity Act lead for Solent NHS Trust in 2010 and has completed a master's degree in mental health law. A key aspect of his current role is to train and support nursing staff in best practice in relation to the Mental Health Act.

Philip Wales is currently a senior manager working for the Care Quality Commission. Between 2004 and 2009 he was employed as a regional director in the Mental Health Act Commission. Before specialising in Mental Health Act regulation Philip held senior management positions within the NHS in the mental health and acute hospital sectors. He qualified as a mental health nurse in 1987 and has undertaken advanced nurse training. He is a trained counsellor and systemic psychotherapist. He has degrees in nursing and complementary health studies.

Foreword

The Mental Health Act is one of the most complex pieces of legislation a mental health nurse is likely to encounter in practice. This complexity is further compounded by the influence of other European and national laws. In such a maelstrom of legal nuance, jargon and ethical dilemma sit some of the most vulnerable people in need of care and compassion, and the challenge of providing person-centred care in this context cannot be overestimated.

In this book Richard Murphy and Philip Wales have provided us with a carefully planned, logical journey through the Mental Health Act from its developmental history to the more recent amendments in 2007. This book effectively de-mystifies the Act, creating a useful guide that will assist in everyday practice. In considering the role the mental health nurse has in the application of the Mental Health Act, the authors have woven the principles underpinning the operation of the Act throughout the book, providing hints and tips, clear concept summaries and even revision questions to aid the reader in expanding not only their understanding of the Act itself, but also the underlying ethical considerations. The outlines of the different roles and responsibilities of professionals operating the Act are also extremely useful.

Whether you are a student approaching mental health law for the first time, a newly qualified nurse about to embark in practice or a practitioner of some years standing wanting to refresh your working knowledge, this book will stand you in good stead. It can be read as a coherent whole or dipped into, section by section, to assist you in practice in an increasingly complex world of mental health care and providing a useful addition to your toolkit to ensure good, defensible, person-centred practice.

Perhaps the most important feature of this book is the fact that the patient is never overlooked. The authors interpret the Act in the way it was designed, to protect and serve individuals temporarily unable to serve themselves. The activities and case studies provide a comprehensive review of the ethical issues raised by the use of such a powerful medium of control in a caring context. It highlights, quite rightly, the difficulties posed for nurses in balancing the needs of the person with the legal requirements of the Act. Engaging with the book will help you to become a more empowered practitioner who is ready to face the ethical dilemmas which will inevitably arise in the care of vulnerable people.

Sandra Walker
Series Editor

Acknowledgements

The authors and publisher would like to thank the Care Quality Commission for allowing use of their data on First Tier (Mental Health) Tribunals (Figures 10.1 and 10.2).

Richard Murphy would like to thank Solent NHS Trust for their support in enabling him to complete the writing of this book. Richard also thanks his family for their support, especially when taking time out on holiday, and acknowledging the gifts of Kath, Rose and John: his wife, daughter and son.

Introduction

About this book

Mental Health Law in Nursing is an essential guide for mental health nursing students to mental health law required for practice, focusing on the Mental Health Act and Code of Practice and the key issues in caring for mental health patients.

Mental health nurses care both for informal patients and for people whose rights are restricted under the Mental Health Act (MHA). Nurses have certain legal duties and obligations towards all patients and there are specific considerations which regulate their care of detained patients. The MHA underwent significant revision in 2007 and a new Code of Practice was published to coincide with the changes to the MHA. It is an essential requirement of their preparation for registration that student mental health nurses have an in-depth understanding of the Mental Health Act to equip them to meet their Code obligations when registered. Mental health nurses also need to understand, and know how to apply, other laws. Together with the MHA these laws create an overarching legal framework. This book, though focusing primarily on the revised MHA and the care of detained patients in particular, will also provide an introduction to the major legal issues that mental health nursing students need to know about, so equipping them to be fit for registration.

In Chapter 1, Mental health nursing and mental health law, the student is introduced to the subject, and the role of the nurse. A brief outline of the history of mental health legislation is followed by a summarising of the key provisions of the MHA and the Code of Practice. The authors emphasise the importance of linking applied knowledge about the Act and the development of core professional standards for registered nurses. There is an introduction to other key legal frameworks for mental health nurses caring for both informal and detained patients.

Chapter 2 is about patients' rights. It outlines the wider legal framework which seeks to protect all patients, including detained patients. It helps the student understand that the rights of patients are governed by a number of laws, not only the MHA. The particular rights and entitlements that both informal and detained patients in particular have are summarised. It also includes a practical guide to informing patients about their rights.

In Chapter 3, Professional roles and responsibilities, there is a description of the roles and responsibilities of all relevant professional groups involved in the operation of the Act at various stages of a patient's pathway. These include the nurse, the approved clinician, the responsible clinician, approved mental health professional (AMHP), second opinion appointed doctors (SOADs), independent mental health act advocates, hospital managers, Mental Health Act managers, mental health tribunals, the police, Ministry of Justice and the Secretary of State.

Chapter 4, Admission and detention in hospital, looks more closely at the various sections of the MHA and Code of Practice which relate to detention under the Act. It explains civil pathways to hospital admission, and covers some of the common problems or issues that nurses encounter when a detained patient is admitted to a ward.

In Chapter 5, Medical treatment for mental disorder, we discuss patient involvement in treatment, whether they be informal or detained patients. This chapter explores Part IV of the MHA with particular emphasis on the nurse's role in the administration of lawfully prescribed treatment for certain groups of detained patients. The chapter guides the reader on the distinctions between lawful and unlawful treatment and gives considerable weight to the Code of Practice provisions, so stressing the nurse's wider duty to uphold good practice, which goes beyond practice that is simply lawful. It makes clear and strong links between the Code and the Nursing and Midwifery Council's (NMC's) standards in relation to administration of medication. The chapter highlights common or recurring problems and offers remedies or actions to address these.

Chapter 6, Leave from hospital, gives a detailed account of the conditions that must be met when granting detained patients leave from hospital. It deals with the different types of leave that can be arranged and makes clear the different responsibilities that nurses and doctors (responsible clinicians) have in relation to leave for detained patients. As with other chapters, some of nurses' commonly encountered difficulties are discussed. The chapter also briefly discusses the issues that arise in regard to informal patients having time out of hospital.

Chapter 7, Supervised community treatment, summarises the new powers that came into force following the amendment to the MHA in 2007. The emerging significance of these powers is discussed as are nurses' particular duties in ensuring that the powers are used both lawfully and are compliant with the Code of Practice. The chapter touches on the ethical/moral concerns about community treatment orders (CTO) and acknowledges the considerable debate about these and the challenge this raises for nurses striving for best practice.

In Chapter 8, Courts and police powers, the main ways in which people can be admitted to hospital via the court or police routes are outlined. The chapter addresses the kinds of facilities in which such people may be cared for (low secure, medium secure, high secure) and deals with particular restrictions on liberty that pertain to people transferred to hospital from prison/courts. The chapter addresses the stigma that patients admitted by these routes can face and the disproportionate admission of certain ethnic groups by these routes. The challenge both of these phenomena poses to nurses is considered.

Chapter 9, Best practice and the Mental Health Act: leadership and care, looks at the various ways the law holds nurses accountable for the patient care they provide. The relationship between this accountability and best practice is explored in the context of the MHA. The offences under the MHA are considered as is the relationship between the MHA and safeguarding vulnerable groups. Finally, the chapter considers the importance of leadership in nursing as a means to protect against care that falls below the standards of best practice.

The role of tribunals and managers' hearings in ensuring there are appropriate safeguards in relation to a patient's detention is explored in Chapter 10. The difference between these two forums is explored, as is the various powers each have. The ways a nurse is likely to be involved in each forum is considered. In particular, the chapter looks at the written and oral evidence a nurse will be expected to give in assisting the two decision making forums.

Requirements for the NMC Standards for Pre-registration Nursing Education and the Essential Skills Clusters

The NMC has established standards of competence to be met by applicants to different parts of the register, and these are the standards it considers necessary for safe and effective practice. In addition to the competencies, the NMC has set out specific skills that nursing students must be able to perform at various points of an education programme. These are known as Essential Skills Clusters (ESCs). This book is structured so that it will help you to understand and meet the competencies and ESCs required for entry to the NMC register. The relevant competencies and ESCs are presented at the start of each chapter so that you can clearly see which ones the chapter addresses. There are *generic standards* that all nursing students irrespective of their field must achieve, and *field-specific standards* relating to each field of nursing, i.e. mental health, children, learning disability and adult nursing. Most chapters have generic standards, and occasionally field-specific standards are listed.

This book includes the latest standards for 2010 onwards, taken from *Standards for Pre-registration Nursing Education* (NMC, 2010).

Learning features

Throughout the book there are activities which challenge you to engage with the issues under discussion. Some activities ask you to reflect on aspects of practice, or your experience of it, or the people or situations you encounter. *Reflection* is an essential skill in nursing, and it helps you to understand the world around you and often to identify how things might be improved. Other activities will help you to develop key skills such as your ability to *think critically* about a topic in order to challenge received wisdom, or your ability to *research a topic and find appropriate information and evidence,* and to be able to make decisions using that evidence in situations that are often difficult and time-pressured. Finally, communication and working as part of a team are core to all nursing practice, and some activities will ask you to carry out *group activities* or think about your *communication skills* to help develop these.

All the activities require you to take a break from reading the text, think through the issues presented and carry out some independent study, possibly using the internet. Where appropriate, there are sample answers presented at the end of each chapter, and these will help you to understand more fully your own reflections and independent study. Remember, academic study will always require independent work; attending lectures will never be enough to be successful on your programme, and these activities will help to deepen your knowledge and understanding of the issues under scrutiny and give you practice at working on your own.

The case studies describe named service users and in several chapters the treatment and recovery journey is followed for one person. For instance, in Chapter 6 you will be asked to reflect on the impact detention can have on a person's life and how leave can be significant in promoting their recovery. You will be assisted in doing this by looking at the case study of a young male who has been detained, the various people who are involved in his leave and the importance of this leave to him. Later in the chapter you will be asked to think about how leave can be a time of risk and how this can be reduced by ensuring there is no ambiguity when planning the place and purpose of leave. The Code of Practice gives guidance on what to consider when planning leave and you will be asked to consider this alongside your own ideas. Often this leave needs to be escorted and hospitals will need to ensure that patients are given equitable access to leave; a scenario demonstrates how patient involvement in the running of the ward can help ensure this occurs. Later on in a person's recovery they may be in a position in which they are having extended periods of leave from the ward. By following James's recovery and preparation to return home you will be supported in considering some of the dilemmas this raises. You will then be asked to consider how research can help nurses and hospitals reduce patients going absent without leave. Finally, you will be introduced to the challenges the case of Melanie Rabone raises for the care of informal patients and the time they have off the ward. In each chapter there are realistic scenarios of nursing care which help you think about situations you may well encounter during your career. There are also research summaries to help you understand important research findings, and concept summaries to provide a grounding in more complex ideas.

You might want to think about completing these activities as part of your personal development plan (PDP) or portfolio. After completing the activity write it up in your PDP or portfolio in a section devoted to that particular skill, then look back over time to see how far you are developing. You can also do more of the activities for a key skill that you have identified a weakness in, which will help build your skill and confidence in this area.

Chapter 1
Mental health nursing and mental health law

continued ...

3. People can trust the newly registered graduate nurse to respect them as individuals and strive to help them to preserve their dignity at all times.

By entry to the register

4. Acts professionally to ensure that personal judgements, prejudices, values, attitudes and beliefs do not compromise care.

Chapter aims

By the end of this chapter you will be able to:

- explain why the law impacts on mental health nursing more than in other fields of nursing;
- describe recent changes in the National Health Service (NHS) approach to caring for people with mental health problems;
- locate the Mental Health Act and the Code and understand how they are used together.

Introduction

The purpose of this chapter will be to help you to understand more about why we have a Mental Health Act (MHA), what that Act deals with and doesn't deal with and how it is implemented. In addition we will take a first look at the Codes of Practice and the *Reference Guide to the Mental Health Act 1983* (Department of Health, 2008a), both important in helping you to navigate your way through the Act. Before we take a look at those issues we shall also discuss mental health nursing, its history and recent developments. In this chapter, and throughout the book, we will emphasise the importance of linking applied knowledge about the Act and the development of core professional standards for registered nurses.

Although throughout this book we shall be mainly discussing the MHA 1983 it is worth pointing out here there are other Acts which are brought to bear on the work of a nurse, these being the Mental Capacity Act 2005 and the Human Rights Act 1998. Both of those Acts will be discussed in more detail in the relevant chapters which follow this one. So let's start by looking at the problems of people who mental health nurses are caring for.

Mental illness and mental health nursing

What is mental illness?

A mental illness is a condition which affects a person's thinking, feelings and their general mood. It can have an impact on relationships with others and day to day living. It is estimated that one in four people in the UK will have a mental health problem during the course of their life, and it can happen at any stage of life. The degree to which it will interfere with someone's home or work life, relationships and general wellbeing vary, depending on a range of factors. However, it will affect some or all of these areas to one degree or another. Depression, schizophrenia and bipolar disorder are amongst the most widely known conditions but there are many other forms of mental illness including anxiety disorders, obsessive compulsive disorder (OCD), eating disorders, post-traumatic stress disorder (PTSD) and personality disorders.

Mental health nursing today

Caring for people with mental health problems is rewarding, but challenging and often complex. Many of the rewards come from dealing with the variety of people you may be called up to care for, ranging from children and young people to adults and older adults. You will of course be caring for people from different social backgrounds, and varying in sexual orientation, gender, ethnicity and race. You will be caring for people in one or more of a wide variety of settings, from different forms of inpatient settings to specialist community mental health services. Although there continues to be an increasing drive towards use of community resources, some of which may be offered in partnership with voluntary and charitable agencies, there is still a need for highly skilled and trained inpatient nursing staff. Wherever care is delivered you will need to work collaboratively with other members of the multidisciplinary team, service users and their carers. As well as being concerned with people's mental health needs, given the interrelationship between different needs, your duty of care also covers their physical, social and spiritual needs.

Activity 1.1   *Communication*

Working collaboratively to promote life choices and positive health outcomes is a key role of the mental health nurse. Think about and list the advantages of referring to those you work with as service users rather than patients and write down why this may be of more significance in the field of mental health.

A brief outline answer to this activity is given at the end of the chapter.

Core aspects of mental health nursing

Mental health nursing is arguably more person centred than other areas of nursing; it relies on the establishment of therapeutic relationships with service users to facilitate change and bring about recovery. It also places considerable value on using thinking skills and critical and analytical thinking, increasing self-understanding. As a result, the ongoing development of what is often referred to as the 'therapeutic use of self' by drawing on your own reflections of your experiences will be crucial to the success of your work with service users and carers. This

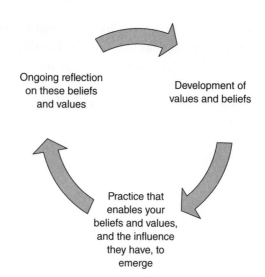

Figure 1.1: The use and development of self in nursing practice.

can only be done through ongoing examination of your own values and beliefs so that any limiting beliefs (prejudices) which get in the way of you being able to respect others are brought into awareness and managed.

Although our knowledge of mental health is continually developing, leading to improvements in care, there is still a great deal which is not known. As such, therefore, mental health nursing is essentially an interdisciplinary profession. Caring for people with a mental illness will require you to draw upon a variety of skills from different interrelated fields including psychology, sociology, psychotherapy and pharmacology. A typical programme of study for someone training to become a mental health nurse is likely to include the following elements:

- A study of health sciences
- Therapeutic relationship
- Caring for those with moderate mental health difficulties
- Nursing those with complex mental health needs
- Managing medicines
- Contemporary mental health policy and legislation
- Management and leadership skills
- Developing critical, analytic and reflective thinking
- Service user and carers' experiences of living with mental health problems
- Evidence based decision making

Some of the elements above may be easily recognisable in your own programme of study but there may be others which seem less obvious. Whatever the particular structure of your own programme those providing it must ensure that they are working to the standards, outcomes and competencies for pre-registration nursing programmes so that you are eligible for registration and fit to practice.

Choose three of the above elements and list a way in which they contribute to the work of a mental health nurse.

A brief outline answer to this activity is given at the end of the chapter.

Recovery based approaches to mental healthcare

One of the major areas of interest and debate in mental health nursing over the last two decades or so has been around the idea of recovery based mental healthcare. It has had a significant influence in the development of mental health policy and is one way through which mental health services are currently being modernised and developed. Essentially, the core idea is that many individuals who experience severe mental illness can develop beyond the initial impact of their mental illness and lead lives which are meaningful. Although there is not one universally accepted definition there a cluster of commonly recognisable features which emerge when engaged in discussions about recovery. These include concepts such as hope, responsibility, positive risk taking, autonomy (self-determination) and control.

Draw a spider diagram on recovery. Include the key ideas and themes that you see are involved in the recovery approach. You may want to keep this diagram and add to it as you learn more about recovery.

A brief outline answer is given at the end of the chapter.

Recovery based approaches emphasise the importance of developing responses to the limiting effects of both the illness that a person experiences and any unwanted effects of the treatment being given within a wider context of understanding a person's unique life circumstances. This then has implications for both you and service users. For mental health nurses it is essential to see individuals with mental health difficulties holistically with their own contribution to make to their recovery. For service users a recovery oriented approach may mean having to review and revise their own beliefs about how they live with illness and start to see themselves as having greater responsibility to manage, with support, their illness and their recovery. This approach holds that those with mental illness should not be stigmatised or discriminated against further by being treated as people who cannot adapt and respond positively as we might expect those with other forms of illness to do. A key consequence of the development of the recovery model is that it has, for mental health nurses, changed the way they conceptualise their role.

Practising lawfully, practising ethically

Though recovery based approaches emphasise participation, engagement and collaboration in care, some of the challenges you will no doubt face when caring for those with mental health needs arise from realising that your duty of care may conflict with an individual's wishes.

Society rightly expects you to provide good, high quality and evidence based care for those with mental health problems. With this comes the notion of the individual's participation, based on their consent, in their care and treatment. Given the nature of mental illness there will inevitably be times when conflict arises because their mental illness may well interfere with their ability to exercise self-determination and autonomy, or the decisions that an individual can make when their thinking is impaired through illness. Your job will be to work as collaboratively with service users as possible and to seek to explain when you can't do this, why and ensure that your actions are lawful.

Scenario

Darren is 23 years old and detained under section 3 with a depressive illness. He is assessed as a high risk of suicide and absconding and currently has no leave to go outside the hospital. In talking to him he expresses to you how important his girlfriend is to him and how down he becomes when he can't see her. He asks you to let him go and see her. You empathise with his distress and frustration and then explain your duty of care to him and that he is only allowed leave in certain circumstances. You look at other ways he can keep in contact and agree to work with him on a recovery care plan of what he needs to be able to do to have leave with his girlfriend.

All of us value our freedom to make choices about how we conduct our lives. Because mental health problems interfere with people's choices and how they wish to live, from time to time their choices may be overridden.

So, mental health legislation marks out how we can interfere with those individual freedoms for those people who may require, but may not see the need to receive, care or treatment for their mental disorder. You will need to be continually aware of this through acknowledging and compensating for the imbalance of power which will exist between you and those experiencing mental health problems.

Section summary

In this section we have taken an overview of the role of the mental health nurse. We have considered the nature of mental illness in a general way and examined the key factors which make up mental health nursing and set it apart from other branches. We have looked too at one of the most recent developments in mental health nursing and its impact on the development of the profession. As we have seen from the foregoing section one of the major differences between mental health nursing and other forms of nursing is that legislation plays a particular role in marking out limits for the care, treatment and control of some of those who experience mental illness.

In the rest of this chapter we shall set out the significance of the MHA in broad terms and its applicability to your work. However, in order for you to be familiar with a number of legal concepts and ideas we shall next outline the process through which laws are made.

A brief guide to the law

It is a requirement of the Nursing and Midwifery Council's (NMC's) standards for pre-registration nursing that you have an understanding of the law and the relevant legal frameworks which govern care. In a companion volume in this series *Law and Professional Issues in Nursing*, Griffith and Tengnah (2010) set out a number of key areas for nursing where an understanding of the law is particularly important. They include: accountability, equality and human rights, consent to treatment, protecting vulnerable adults and children, negligence, record keeping, confidentiality and health and safety. Their schema is not definitive, but it is extensive and shows you just how much the law impacts on the practice of nursing today.

As you work through the subsequent chapters of this book you will see that many of the themes which they address will also be dealt with here as they apply particularly to those with mental health problems.

Activity 1.4   *Reflection*

Before continuing, stop and think about some of the laws that you are aware of. Next think about whether you can identify how these laws came into existence. Once you have done this, read on and compare your observations with the discussion below.

There is no outline answer given for this activity.

Types of legislative process

In the UK there are essentially three ways in which new laws come into being: through Acts of Parliament (statute), by secondary legislation and by common law (case law). But whichever way a law comes to be made there is no distinction between the mechanism through which a law becomes a law and the degree to which it demands obedience. Alongside the laws themselves there are codes, guides, commentaries and analysis of the laws, all of which are designed to assist us to understand and apply the law correctly to a given situation. Mental health legislation is one which is full of commentary and opinion about the operation of the law itself, as you will see.

Acts of Parliament

These are statute laws and are sometimes referred to as 'primary legislation'. Before an Act is passed, a bill (which is a draft form of the intended Act) passes through a number of stages in both Houses of Parliament. These stages involve debate, scrutiny and amendments to the bill by both Houses in turn. Once the bill has been approved by both Houses the bill then receives Royal Assent. For a bill to become an Act it must have been approved by both Houses of Parliament. It can begin its passage through Parliament in either House. For example, the MHA 2007 (which amended the 1983 Act) began its journey in the House of Lords rather than Commons.

Case study: amending the MHA 1983

A summary of the key dates marking the progress of the Mental Health Bill which became the MHA 2007 which amended the MHA 1983.

Progress through the House of Lords

First reading: 16 November 2006

Second reading: 28 November 2006

Committee stage: 8–29 January 2007

Report stage: 19–27 February 2007

Third reading: 6 March 2007

Progress through the House of Commons

First reading: 7 March 2007

Second reading: 16 April 2007

Committee stage: 24 April–15 May 2007

Report stage: 18–19 June 2007

Third reading: 19 June 2007

Royal Assent: 19 July 2007

Although Parliament is the main law making body for the UK, two developments have had an effect on the reach of UK law. First, as a member of the European Union (EU) the UK has signed various treaties giving EU law precedence over UK law where the EU has made laws (which are called directives). Second, power is devolved to national assemblies in Northern Ireland, Scotland and Wales, each now having law making powers which differ between each of those countries.

Secondary legislation

If changes to primary legislation are needed, one way of achieving this is through the creation of secondary legislation. There are a number of forms which secondary legislation can take. The most widely known is called a statutory instrument. Their use means that Parliament does not need to pass a new Act as instead a government minister can make more detailed regulations (laws). This is achieved by having included in the relevant Act a clear framework which enables amendment to the Act.

Case study: statute law and secondary legislation: the Health and Social Care Act 2008

The Health and Social Care Act (2008) was given Royal Assent on 21 July 2008 having gone through the stages outlined above. This Act led to the creation of the Care Quality Commission whose role is to inspect health and social care providers and make judgements about their compliance with the various rules (regulations) which they have to follow as a condition of their registration and their licence to operate. However, Parliament chose not to put the detailed list of regulated activities which care services now follow in the Act itself. Instead these were enacted through a process of secondary legislation. The Health and Social Care Act 2008 (Registration of Regulated Activities) Regulations 2009 was made on 11 March 2009 and came into force on 1 April of that year.

Of course not all Acts of Parliament will make provision for secondary legislation to be enacted through forms of secondary legislation, but many will.

Common law

Common law is also referred to as 'case law'. It is law which has been made by judges making rulings in particular cases that then apply to all other cases which are considered to be the same, ensuring consistent judgement being uniformly applied in different parts of the country. Although case law by its nature is born out of the consideration of the details of one particular matter the judgements become binding on other, lower, courts. The most senior court in the UK is the Supreme Court and beneath it the Court of Appeal and then the High Court. The benefit of this system is that it leads to consistency of application of the law once a difficult issue has been aired before it. However, the alleged similarities and differences between cases once a judgement has been made gives rise to further precedent and further judgements being made, each building up the body of case law on a particular topic. In the field of mental health, for example, one authoritative source lists over 1200 cases which have something to say about the operation of the MHA. Though you may wish to study case law in detail it is generally sufficient to be aware of the idea of precedent, that is, case law will affect the way in which the MHA operates because it changes some aspects of it. You will learn more about this in later chapters. Having reviewed the processes by which laws become made we now turn to look at the history of mental health legislation.

A brief history of mental health legislation

The purpose of this section is to set out some of the fundamental changes which have occurred in mental health law in the last 300 or so years in the UK. There is a list of useful websites and selected reading at the end of this chapter if you wish to look at this particular subject in more detail.

Whose history?

The study of the history of mental healthcare and its attendant legislation fall within the fields of social and cultural history. There are different perspectives which historians will bring to the subject: a focus on notable individuals and their influence on mental healthcare (such as, for example, Philippe Pinel or William Tuke), studying service users' histories, and the history of medical and scientific discoveries, to name just a few. This is to be expected as historians choose to examine events from any number of different perspectives which will each lead to different narratives or emphases. These different views often complement, overlap and even sometimes contradict one another.

In their book *Mental Health Law in England and Wales,* Barber et al. (2012) describe significant legislative 'milestones', summarised in Table 1.1.

The nineteenth and twentieth centuries have seen many Acts of Parliament which legislate detention, classification, monitoring and protecting the rights of those subject to detention. The most recent changes to the MHA came about in 2007 following a very long process of consultation and parliamentary debate which included the earlier drafting of two bills which were both abandoned. The result was that in 2007 a series of changes were made to the 1983 Act which left considerable parts of it unchanged but introduced a small number of new powers and procedures.

Legislative changes are useful waymarkers in the history of mental healthcare itself. The last 200 years or so have also seen both the creation and then the gradual dismantling of a system of mental healthcare which was based on the model of the county asylum. We see from the

Year	Act	Comment
1713–44	Vagrancy Acts	Allowed detention of 'Lunaticks or mad persons'
1774	Act for regulating private madhouses	
1845	Lunatics Act	Included 'Person of unsound mind'
1886	Idiots Act	Provided separately for idiots and imbeciles
1890	Lunacy (Consolidation) Act	Ignored the distinction
1913	Mental Deficiency Act	Typology and segregation of 'mental defectives'
1927	Mental Deficiency Act	Emphasised the need for care outside the institution
1930	Mental Treatment Act	Allowed for voluntary admissions. This was the first time that it was considered that anyone might actually want to be admitted to a psychiatric hospital without coercion
1946	NHS Act	
1959	MHA	
1983	MHA	
2007	MHA (Amendment)	Amended the 1983 Act

Table 1.1: Legislative milestones.

above that legislation to address the needs of the mentally ill is something which has undergone periodic review and development in response to both social change and our developing understanding of treatments.

In the last century the most notable changes were introduced in 1959 but the roots of that change lay in the previous decade. Following the establishment of the NHS came the realisation that caring for those with mental health and learning difficulties in large mental institutions was expensive. As a result, and taken together with ongoing changes in social attitudes towards the mentally ill, came the need to look again at the way in which care was provided. The then new Act was developed in response to an earlier extensive Royal Commission (the Percy Commission). This Commission made a number of recommendations, among them the need to treat people on a voluntary basis as far as possible, that mental health hospitals (then commonly referred to as mental institutions) should be managed in the same way as general hospitals, and local authorities should play a greater role in providing residential and other services so that only those who needed treatment should be in hospital.

Having looked at the way in which laws are made and carried out a review of the history of mental health legislation, we turn next to start looking more closely at the current MHA.

Introducing the MHA 1983

You might have noticed the Act's length, its detail and the formality of the language used. It is written in a style which is quite different from that which we would see in other documents. It has ten major parts within the main body of the Act as well as some supplementary schedules. The MHA 1983 contained 149 different sections but a closer look will tell you that there are more than this, as the 2007 MHA (which amended the 1983 Act) introduced a number of additional sections which have been inserted and assigned letters (for example sections 17A–17G) followed by six further schedules.

Having looked at the Act you may be somewhat relieved to discover that it is not necessary to be familiar with all of its provisions. This is because, as you may have already noticed, it is concerned with a series of technical matters not all of which will be of direct applicability to your nursing work. As a result, this book will not discuss all of the parts of the Act but is necessarily selective. It focuses on those which will be more immediately relevant to nursing. What is intended rather is that you will have a working knowledge of the Act as it generally applies to mental health nurses. So, where the Act seems to speak more to other groups of professionals (such as Part VIII which deals with 'miscellaneous functions' of local authorities and the Secretary of State) then we shall not discuss those areas other than to touch on them.

Code of Practice to the MHA

We have seen that the MHA is long, complex and, in places, difficult to understand. To help you apply the law correctly the Act has also, alongside it, a Code of Practice. With the updating of the MHA in 2007 the Code of Practice was also updated. One significant difference here was the creation of a separate Code of Practice for England. As you will see as we refer to either or both Codes throughout this book, the two Codes are similar in many respects, as for example in the statement of guiding principles (Chapter 2) these are highlighted as appropriate. You will, for the most part, need only to become familiar with one or other Code during the course of your work, but it is nonetheless important to be aware of the existence of both.

Activity 1.6   *Critical thinking*

Obtain a copy of either one of the Codes or Practice (England/Wales). As you did for the MHA, examine its contents and explore some of the chapters. Again, make some notes on your observations then read the following section and compare your response with that below.

There is no outline answer provided for this activity.

Arranged in chapters related to the Act, the Code sets out, in considerable detail, guidance on how to operate the Act. You will notice that it has been written in a more accessible style with the intention of it being used day to day as a handbook for anyone involved in operating the Act. It expands on the points of law in the Act as well as regulations (secondary legislation) which have been prepared to deal with further particular circumstances, such as those relating to conflicts of interest (England: Chapter 7; Wales: Chapter 3).

The MHA requires certain groups of professionals to have regard to the Code of Practice when making decisions under the Act. Nurses are one of those groups. It is therefore important that you are familiar with how to use this resource. In Chapter 8, you will also read how more recent case law places emphasis on the importance of the guidance in the Code concerned with further restrictions on detained patients.

Reference Guide to the Mental Health Act 1983

Another helpful companion document to the Mental Health Act is the *Reference Guide to the Mental Health Act 1983* (Department of Health, 2008a). This document explains the Act and secondary legislation related to the Act. Significantly there is no similar document which has been prepared for use within Wales which means that it can only be used therefore where the way in which the Act is used in Wales is directly relevant to its use in England. The Reference Guide describes itself as setting out the main provisions of the Act and sets itself apart from the Code of Practice by emphasising its role of being more concerned with how to apply the Act. However, on viewing the Reference Guide and the Code of Practice alongside each other sometimes this distinction is not as clear-cut as it may sound. There is no duty to have regard to the Reference Guide. However, if there is doubt about how to proceed it is a useful tool to help ensure your practice is lawful.

Section summary

This section has introduced the MHA and begun to look at its key contents. Some of these will be explored in more detail in the coming chapters. It also introduced the Code of Practice and the *Reference Guide to the Mental Health Act* and explained the legal status and usefulness of these.

Chapter summary

This chapter has introduced the professions and social influences in which the MHA is set. The importance of understanding the legislation in light of the recovery approach has been stressed and you have been introduced to how laws are made and the different types of law. Some of the contents of the MHA have been introduced as has the Code of Practice and the Reference Guide.

Activities: brief outline answers

Activity 1.1

The term patient can imply a passive recipient of something being done to them by an expert. It can reinforce inequality in power in decision making. 'Service user' implies a more collaborative approach and a person who uses services that you offer, as a part of their life. It may be more important in mental health because, as the recovery approach sets out, positive mental health is intimately connected to our own meaning, hope and self-determination. Also, in mental health, service users can be subject to considerable coercion under the MHA.

Activity 1.2

These are some examples of how you could have answered.

- A study of health sciences: each discipline will have its own way to conceptualise situations that will enable interventions that bring about different types of change.
- Therapeutic relationship: through forming therapeutic relationships patients can powerfully experience hope, strength and belief in positive future outcomes.
- Managing medicines: medication can be an important way in which service users start to take control of their own symptoms.
- Contemporary mental health policy and legislation: knowledge of this area can ensure that coercion is only used when it is lawful to do so.
- Management and leadership skills: developing these skills is key to ensuring a mental health service that safeguards the rights of patients and provides quality care (see Chapter 9).
- Developing critical, analytic and reflective thinking: developing these skills is essential in understanding power relationships, how our own beliefs and values impact upon our interventions and developing ourselves as a resource.

- Service user and carers' experiences of living with mental health problems: developing methods to promote and ensure service user involvement can ensure services are developed collaboratively and can prevent misuse of power.
- Evidence based decision making: this is essential to ensure that methods of interventions used actually achieve the positive outcomes that are sought.

Activity 1.3

Here are some ideas you may have had for your spider diagram.

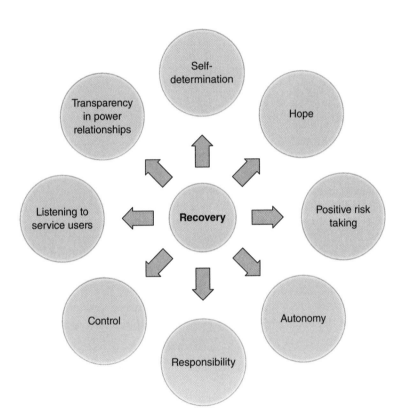

Figure 1.2: Recovery.

Further reading

Coleman, R, Baker, P and Taylor, K (2000) *Working to Recovery: Victim to victor III, a guide to mental wellbeing.* Gloucester: Handsell Publishing.

A good starting point to understand how the recovery approach can change our understanding of mental wellbeing and empower service users.

Porter, R (2002) *Madness: A brief history.* Oxford: Oxford University Press.

Great starting point for understanding how perceptions of mental illness have changed throughout time.

Useful websites

http://www.parliament.uk/about/how/laws/passage-bill

This website explains the passage of a bill through Parliament.

Multiple choice questions

1. In which year was the current Mental Health Act originally made law?

   (a)   1970
   (b)   1983
   (c)   2007
   (d)   2001

2. Who enacts primary legislation?

   (a)   The monarch (the king or queen)
   (b)   Judges in a court of law
   (c)   Parliament
   (d)   The police

3. In which year did the law first allow for voluntary admission to mental hospitals?

   (a)   1924
   (b)   2004
   (c)   1930
   (d)   1830

4. What is the name of the document which you have to help you in your application of the Mental Health Act?

   (a)   *Reference Guide to the Mental Health Act 1983*
   (b)   *Reference Book for the Mental Health Act*
   (c)   *Code of Conduct for Nurses*
   (d)   *Mental Health Act Code of Practice*

Chapter 2
Patients' rights

NMC Standards for Pre-registration Nursing Education

This chapter will address the following competencies:

Domain 1: Professional values

2. All nurses must practise in a holistic, non-judgmental, caring and sensitive manner that avoids assumptions, supports social inclusion; recognises and respects individual choice; and acknowledges diversity. Where necessary, they must challenge inequality, discrimination and exclusion from access to care.

2.1. Mental health nurses must practise in a way that addresses the potential power imbalances between professionals and people experiencing mental health problems, including situations when compulsory measures are used, by helping people exercise their rights, upholding safeguards and ensuring minimal restrictions on their lives. They must have an in depth understanding of mental health legislation and how it relates to care and treatment of people with mental health problems.

3. All nurses must support and promote the health, wellbeing, rights and dignity of people, groups, communities and populations. These include people whose lives are affected by ill health, disability, inability to engage, ageing or death. Nurses must act on their understanding of how these conditions influence public health.

3.1. Mental health nurses must promote mental health and wellbeing, while challenging the inequalities and discrimination that may arise from or contribute to mental health problems.

Domain 2: Communication and interpersonal skills

2. All nurses must use a range of communication skills and technologies to support person-centred care and enhance quality and safety. They must ensure people receive all the information they need in a language and manner that allows them to make informed choices and share decision making. They must recognise when language interpretation or other communication support is needed and know how to obtain it.

8. All nurses must respect individual rights to confidentiality and keep information secure and confidential in accordance with the law and relevant ethical and regulatory frameworks, taking account of local protocols. They must also actively share personal information with others when the interests of safety and protection override the need for confidentiality.

NMC Essential Skills Clusters

This chapter will address the following ESCs:

Cluster: Care, compassion and communication

4. People can trust a newly qualified graduate nurse to engage with them and their family or carers within their cultural environments in an acceptant and anti-discriminatory manner free from harassment and exploitation.

By the first progression point

2. Respects people's rights.

By the third progression point

4. Upholds people's legal rights and speaks out when these are at risk of being compromised.

7. People can trust the newly registered graduate nurse to protect and keep as confidential all information relating to them.

By the first progression point

1. Applies the principles of confidentiality.

By the third progression point

8. Works within the legal frameworks for data protection including access to and storage of records.

9. Acts within the law when confidential information has to be shared with others.

Cluster: Organisational aspects of care

11. People can trust the newly registered graduate nurse to safeguard children and adults from vulnerable situations and support and protect them from harm.

By the third progression point

9. Supports people in asserting their human rights.

Chapter aims

By the end of this chapter you will be able to:

- understand the importance of essential human rights to the practice of mental health nursing;
- describe some of the values which underpin essential human rights;
- outline factors which may work against respecting the rights of others;
- summarise key patient rights;
- describe your role under the Mental Health Act around explaining rights to detained patients.

Introduction

Case study: room for improvement?

Sian Pendry arrived on St Donat's Ward at about 9 a.m. on Monday morning to begin her Mental Health Act (MHA) monitoring visit on behalf of Healthcare Inspectorate Wales. St Donat's Ward rarely cares for patients detained under the MHA but Mr Nevin Swancott had been admitted under section 4 on Saturday evening. Another patient had been discharged from section 3 several days ago but remained on the ward as an informal patient. Sian spoke to Mr Swancott and asked him what he knew about his rights as a detained patient. He said that although another patient had tried to be helpful, the leaflet she had shown him from the Care Quality Commission (CQC) about electro-convulsive therapy (ECT) had frightened him. Later the nurse in charge confirmed that ward practice was that patients were always informed, initially, of their rights under the MHA by an MHA administrator in the presence of a nurse. A previous complaints investigation had found that nurses had been giving incorrect information to patients about their rights and this practice had been recommended following that investigation.

Activity 2.1   *Critical thinking*

Thinking specifically about informing patients of their rights under the MHA, what do you think might be some of the areas for practice development for the nursing team on St Donat's Ward?

An outline answer is given at the end of the chapter.

This chapter looks in detail at the issue of patients' rights, particularly the rights of detained patients under the MHA. It will be important for you to be able to know the specific rights or entitlements that detained patients have as well as your professional duty to help these patients act on those rights. Before we discuss those in detail, however, it's important that we explore some of the surrounding landscape. So, this chapter begins with a discussion of human rights and the values on which basic human rights are founded. It then considers current UK law. The focus then narrows to an overview of specific rights to which all patients are entitled and then onto a consideration of the particular rights of detained patients. By approaching our topic in this way you will see that the rights of mental health patients (whether they are informal or detained) are governed by a number of laws and the MHA, important though it is, is only one part of this much broader rights framework.

An introduction to human rights

Human rights for all

Human rights are the essential freedoms which belong to each of us; to you, to me, to our families, our neighbours, our friends, everyone. So, they belong to every patient that you will care for throughout your career. As a nurse you have to ensure that patients' rights are upheld but there may be times or situations when you may find it less straightforward than it might appear to put this into practice. You may find yourself holding beliefs or attitudes which act as a barrier to respecting and upholding the rights of others. It's important to become aware of your own barriers so that they don't interfere with your duty to ensure that a patient's rights are protected at all times. We will look a little more closely at these barriers next.

Barriers to respecting rights

Barriers can occur when we are presented with a situation which challenges our working assumptions, or core beliefs, about what constitutes fairness, justice or equality. For example, we may believe in fair treatment for everyone, but deep down hold an opposing view that some groups in society are less deserving of fair treatment. We may believe that those imprisoned for sexual offences against children should not be segregated from other prisoners and so be left exposed to the risk of retribution from other inmates. Our values or specifically our prejudices (or preconceived opinions) about individuals or groups of people can, and do, influence our views about whether a given human rights issue seems just. If not made conscious, our values can, however, lead to our being complicit in the limiting of people's rights. Worse still we may believe (wrongly) that human rights favour those who we may believe are 'less deserving' than others. The Equality and Human Rights Commission's recent inquiry into the Human Rights Act found that 42 per cent of people agreed with the proposition that 'the only people to benefit from human rights in the UK are criminals and terrorists'. Negative beliefs about the subject and incorrect and sometimes sensational reporting by the media can lead us to make snap judgements about the importance of human rights.

We each, as nurses, have a wider professional duty to our patients which requires us to continually examine our beliefs so that we do not discriminate against or treat unfavourably the patients in our care irrespective of our personal views about an individual. We are called to practise in 'a holistic, non-judgemental caring and sensitive manner that avoids assumptions'. But we can only practise in a holistic manner if we first become aware of our core beliefs, our assumptions, and reflect on the degree to which they may hinder our ability to care for our patients because they mean that we view one group of people differently from another. Consider, for example, the following case study drawn from a Fitness to Practice hearing conducted at the Nursing and Midwifery Council (NMC) in 2011.

Case study: fitness to practice impaired

Nurse J worked as a mental health nurse. Her fitness to practice was called into question following an allegation that she had acted in a racially abusive manner towards a patient. The patient was being cared for in a secure facility pending the conclusion of inquiries regarding their legal right to stay in the UK. Evidence was heard by the NMC's Fitness to Practice Committee which judged that, on the balance of probabilities, the nurse had failed in her professional obligation to practise in a non-discriminatory way. Sanctions were imposed on the nurse's registration.

Activity 2.2 | *Reflection*

Think about two or three situations where you have experienced negative feelings about people that you have been caring for because of something they have done, the lifestyle they lead or a view they have expressed to you. Without disclosing any personal, confidential information set down your recollections in the following way. 'I remember when I was caring for Mr/Ms … and they said/did …' 'What I found difficult about this at the time was …' Then, 'As I think about this now this tells me … about myself.' Review your notes and consider whether you've identified any themes or barriers that might hinder you from fulfilling your professional obligations towards patients. You may find it helpful to make a commitment to discuss your reflections with a colleague or one of your course tutors.

As this activity is for your own reflection and development there is no outline answer given.

Values based human rights

Activity 2.3 | *Reflection*

Allow 5–10 minutes to mull over the values that you bring to your work as a student mental health nurse. When you have completed your list, compare it with that at the end of this chapter. In comparing your list with that given, does anything particularly stand out for you?

An outline answer is given at the end of the chapter.

In *Whose Values? A workbook for values-based practice in mental health care* (2004), Woodbridge and Fulford recognise that agreeing on what are 'good' or 'right' values is not always easy. The exercise you have just completed may have demonstrated this to you. Working in a respectful way with people who hold different values (whether they are patients, carers or even other staff members) can therefore be challenging. Through a continual process of reflection on your own values and their impact (positive and negative) on your patients, you can remain focused on being patient- (rather than self-) centred.

You can relate to the subject of human rights by thinking about the values that underpin them, making them become more immediate and accessible. One list of core values or principles is that encapsulated by the acronym FREDA:

- Fairness
- Respect
- Equality
- Dignity
- Autonomy

(Department of Health, 2007)

Principles underpinning the operation of the MHA

Within the UK, during the last decade, our increasing focus on human rights has had an impact on the development of the MHA. When it was revised in 2008 a new section (s118 (2a)) was written into the Act which made it a legal requirement that each of the Codes should include a statement of guiding principles which should be considered by anyone making a decision under the Act. Some of these can be easily understood as values, but others require a closer look. They are listed in Table 2.1.

The English Code	The Welsh Code
• Purpose	• Empowerment
• Least restriction	• Equity
• Respect	• Effectiveness
• Participation	• Efficiency
• Effectiveness, efficiency and equity	

Table 2.1: Guiding principles.

Activity 2.4   *Reflection*

Select either the Code for England or that for Wales (see Useful websites) and review Chapter 1 which discusses these guiding principles, some of which refer to one or more of the FREDA values above. Make brief notes as you read through to help you identify which values are highlighted in the Codes' principles. What, if anything, surprises you from your review of the chapter?

As this activity is for your own reflection and development there is no outline answer given.

Section summary

Rights are important to everyone. All people have values which may, in certain circumstances, lead to actions which interfere with the rights of others. Problems for nurses can arise when personal values conflict with our wider professional duty to respect and uphold patients' rights. One of your professional obligations as a mental health nurse will be to develop self-awareness of your core values and reflect on these so that they do not create barriers to delivering effective care.

Having considered the values on which human rights are based we now turn to examine the legislative basis on which our rights in the UK are founded.

Human rights and equality legislation

Human Rights Act 1998

Two major international developments at the end of the Second World War (1939–45) led to the Human Rights Act (HRA) in the UK. Both of these developments were an international response to the atrocity of the Holocaust in which more than six million people were murdered because of their faith, their ethnicity or a disability. The first was the United Nations Universal Declaration of Human Rights which was adopted by the United Nations (UN) General Council in 1948. The second, the European Convention on Human Rights (ECHR), an international agreement (treaty) between European nations, came into force in 1953.

Through these agreements world leaders set down the specific rights of all people throughout the world. By doing so, they sought explicitly to state the limits of a country's intrusion into the lives of its people.

Even though the UK was one of the founding members of the Council of Europe it was not until some 40 years later that the HRA 1998 came into force, so writing the Council's Convention rights into UK law. Before the passage of that Act the only redress available to UK citizens was to take their case to the European Court of Human Rights based in Strasbourg. But now human rights issues can be dealt with through UK courts and tribunals. Amongst other things, the HRA makes it a legal requirement for public authorities (such as government departments, local authorities, National Health Service (NHS) trusts, police, prison, courts and tribunals) to uphold the Convention.

Absolute and non-absolute rights

The HRA (and the Convention) is concerned with two kinds of rights: absolute and non-absolute rights. Non-absolute rights are subdivided further into either 'qualified' or 'limited' rights. An absolute right is one which cannot be infringed under any circumstances but a non-absolute right may, by definition, be restricted. A (non-absolute) qualified right is one where the government can lawfully interfere but only if certain conditions are met. Such interference must be lawful, done to secure a permissible aim (for example for the prevention of crime), is necessary in a democratic society and is proportionate to the threat that other rights might be being put at risk. A qualified right will be subject to restriction when the exercise of that right may conflict with the human rights of others or duty to safeguard the person. A (non-absolute) limited right is one which is restricted in a more explicit way.

Activity 2.5 *Critical thinking*

Review Schedule 1 of the Human Rights Act 1998 (see Useful websites). If human rights are considered fundamental, why do you think that some can be qualified or limited?

An outline answer is given at the end of the chapter.

An important consequence of the HRA is that all UK legislation must now be enacted in such a way that it is compatible with the Convention. But, rather than redraft all current UK legislation it is expected that legislation should be read or interpreted in such a way that it is compatible with the HRA. There will be rare occasions where it is not possible to interpret legislation in this way. When this occurs the legislation is declared incompatible and it is up to Parliament to amend the law. Such declarations are very rare (about three a year) but they can lead to significant changes to the law including the MHA. We shall return to the theme of incompatibility when we look at the rights of 'detained' patients further on.

Equality Act 2010

A second major piece of legislation governing society's approach to rights is the Equality Act 2010. This Act brings together a number of equality and anti-discrimination laws that have been added to the statute books since the mid-1970s. It has replaced the Equal Pay Act 1970; the Sex Discrimination Acts 1975 and 1986; the Race Relations Act 1976; the Disability Discrimination Act 1995; part of the Equality Act 2006; and various Employment Equality Regulations.

By repealing or revoking these and other laws the Equality Act modernises, strengthens and simplifies the law in this area. Two important changes are the introduction of the concept of the protected characteristic and extending the scope of prohibited conduct (forms of discrimination), which we now look at in more detail

Protected characteristics

Prior to the introduction of the Equality Act reference was commonly made to the 'grounds' on which someone required protection from discrimination (such as on the grounds of race, sex, etc.). This Act moves away from 'grounds' and introduces the concept of a 'protected characteristic'. There are nine:

- age;
- disability;
- gender reassignment;
- marriage and civil partnership;
- pregnancy and maternity;
- race;
- religion or belief;
- sex;
- sexual orientation.

As you might expect, these protected characteristics are further defined or qualified within the Act so as to set out the legal basis on which each of these terms is to be used (s12 Equality Act 2010).

Discrimination (prohibited conduct)

Discrimination means treating someone unfavourably on the basis of their 'protected characteristic'.

Case study: counsellor dismissed for refusing to treat gay couples

A relationship counsellor was lawfully dismissed for refusing to treat gay couples and had his appeal for unfair dismissal rejected by an employment tribunal. The counsellor said that encouraging gay sex went against his religious beliefs and so felt that he could not treat same-sex couples. The employment tribunal ruled that he did not have a claim of unfair dismissal as he was sacked because his employers claimed that he would not comply with its policies about treating clients. His employers told the tribunal that they would have treated anyone in the same way, regardless of whether a person held religious beliefs or not.

The protection that the Equality Act offers is wider in scope than the legislation that it replaced. For example, employers' liability to protect their staff or customers from harassment by a third party previously applied only to sex discrimination. Now it has been extended to cover age, disability, gender reassignment, race, religion or belief and sexual orientation. For example, a nursing home manager could be liable if a subcontractor carrying out repairs at the home insults patients in a racially offensive manner. There are seven types of discrimination:

- *Direct discrimination – someone is treated less favourably than another person because of a protected characteristic.*
- *Discrimination by association – direct discrimination against someone because they associate with another person who possesses a protected characteristic.*
- *Discrimination by perception – direct discrimination against someone because others think that they possess a particular protected characteristic.*
- *Indirect discrimination – when you have a rule or policy that applies to everyone but disadvantages a person with a particular protected characteristic.*
- *Harassment – this is behaviour that is deemed offensive by the recipient.*
- *Harassment by a third party – for example employers being potentially liable for the harassment of their staff or customers by people they don't themselves employ, i.e. a contractor.*
- *Victimisation – this occurs when someone is treated badly because they have made or supported a complaint or grievance under this legislation.*

(ACAS, 2010)

It is important to appreciate the significance of the changes to recent legislation so that you do not discriminate against someone inadvertently.

Section summary

Human rights are protected in law by the HRA. Some human rights are absolute, such as the prohibition of torture; others are limited or qualified because the rights of one person has to be balanced against the rights of others or duty to safeguard the person. The Equality Act is also an important statute in protecting people's right to fair treatment. It has strengthened the scope of anti-discrimination legislation so that new forms of discrimination have become prohibited. Together, both Human Rights and Equality legislation provide the legal basis on which the fundamental rights of individuals and groups within society are defended.

Patients' rights

Having reviewed the values underpinning rights and looked at the current legislative frameworks which protect those rights, we now turn to patients' rights. This section is in two parts. We shall look first at the general rights that apply to all patients, irrespective of their circumstances. The remaining part of this chapter will then look at the particular rights that 'detained' patients have and your duties towards them.

General rights

Activity 2.6	*Critical thinking*

Make a list of the essential rights that you think are common to all patients. Now read on and compare your response to that given below.

The Department of Health has, over several decades, launched a number of policy initiatives which have sought to set out patients' rights. The *NHS Constitution for England* (Department of Health, 2010a) is the most recent development. As a result of the devolution settlement, the way that NHS-funded care is delivered and regulated throughout the UK now differs between nations. You can find its source in the list of Useful websites. It contains two kinds of rights. The first are legal rights that apply to all patients regardless of where, and by whom, their care is provided in the UK. Because the document is one for patients in England it also lists a number of other additional pledges which relate to specific entitlements for patients receiving NHS-funded provision in England only.

Right of access to health services	• The right not to be unlawfully discriminated against in the provision of services including on grounds of gender, race, religion or belief, sexual orientation, disability (including learning disability or mental illness) or age.
Quality of care	• The right to be treated with a professional standard of care, by appropriately qualified and experienced staff.
Respect, consent and confidentiality	• The right to be treated with dignity and respect, in accordance with human rights. • The right to accept or refuse treatment and not to be given any physical examination or treatment without valid consent. (Where a patient lacks capacity consent must be obtained from a person legally able to act on their behalf, or the treatment must be in their best interests.) • The right to be given information about proposed treatment in advance, including any significant risks and any alternative treatments which may be available, and the risks involved in doing nothing.

	• The right to privacy and confidentiality and to expect confidential information to be kept safe and secure. • The right of access to health records.
Involvement in healthcare	• The right to be involved in discussions and decisions about healthcare and to be given information to enable this. • The right to be involved, directly or through representatives, in the planning of healthcare services, the development and consideration of proposals for changes in the way those services are provided, and in decisions to be made affecting the operation of those services.
Complaint and redress	• The right to have any complaint dealt with efficiently and to have it properly investigated. • The right to know the outcome of any investigation into a complaint. • The right to compensation if harmed by negligent treatment.

Table 2.2: Summary of patients' rights.

Source: NHS Constitution for England, 2010.

Patients' rights are a set of legally enforceable entitlements for all people who receive care or treatment in the UK. The legal basis for these rights is derived from a number of different statutes and laws (e.g. Data Protection Act 1998 or the common law of negligence). But there are further protections, or rights, that 'detained' patients are entitled to and we now turn to these.

Additional rights for people subject to the MHA

The purpose of the MHA is to provide necessary care and treatment to people suffering from a mental health problem and who would otherwise not receive it unless they were detained. It achieves this objective by limiting, or restricting, the freedoms (rights) that people who are detained have so that they do not put their own or others' rights at risk. For example, the act of detention means that a person's Article 5 right to liberty has been restricted. There are corresponding entitlements that detained patients have to ensure that their human rights are properly safeguarded and that no breach of their human rights occurs.

In this section we shall first give an overview of the rights that those who are subject to the powers of the MHA have. Most of these rights apply in the majority of cases, but not all of the rights under the MHA apply to all patients who come under its scope. For example not all detained patients have a statutory right of access to an independent mental health advocate (IMHA). After summarising the key rights that patients have under the MHA we shall then discuss some ways in which these rights have been amended or developed through a series of case studies. Doing this will help you to know the specific rights themselves and it will help you to see how the HRA (discussed above) as a 'living instrument' exerts its effect on other statutes and specifically in our case the MHA.

Summary of rights for detained patients

The MHA places a specific duty on personnel to inform all patients to whom the Act applies (whether detained, subject to community treatment order or subject to guardianship) about a number of matters, including particular rights. Sections 130D, 132 and 132A of the MHA set out those legal responsibilities. In summary these are:

- to inform a patient as soon as practicable that they are subject to the powers of the Act;
- to take practical steps to ensure that patients understand the information given to them.

Patients should always be told:

- which of the provisions of the MHA apply and their effect;
- their right to appeal against their section (where applicable);
- about the way the powers of the Act are monitored (by the CQC in England or in Wales by Healthcare Inspectorate Wales);
- their right to make a complaint about the use of the MHA;
- how they may be discharged from their order;
- to request to see a copy of the applicable 'Code of Practice' to the MHA.

And, as far as this information is relevant to the patient's circumstances, they should be told:

- the restrictions on their nearest relative applying for their discharge (see Chapter 3);
- how the 'consent to treatment' provisions apply in their case (see Chapter 5);
- their right to see an independent mental health advocate (see Chapter 3);

Patients who come under the powers of the MHA have a right to be given this information both orally and in writing.

You should be aware that the MHA itself is not the only place where this information can be found. Other important places include: the Codes of Practice for England and Wales, Department of Health and NHS Wales. Their websites have model patient information leaflets. The CQC (England) produces a limited number of leaflets as does Healthcare Inspectorate Wales (see Useful websites).

As you will discover some of the documentation produced relating to the MHA has forms of words which cannot be altered or changed. The wording of patient information leaflets though not prescribed by law should always include the minimum requirements in each case.

Throughout this book you will notice that there are other, particular rights which apply to some groups of patients who come under the powers of the MHA. Because of this, it is very important that you always refer to the relevant Code and other guidance when you encounter an unfamiliar situation.

Activity 2.7   *Evidence based practice and research*

Examine a copy of the model patient information leaflet for patients detained under section 2 (see Useful websites). Check whether model information sheets are being used in your local mental health service or if they have been adapted. If so try to find out the reasons why changes have been made, what additional information has been included and see whether they meet the minimum requirements in the model information sheet.

As this activity requires local research there is no outline answer given.

Helping people understand their rights under the MHA

You have an absolutely key role in helping people to understand and exercise the rights that they have under the MHA. For this reason both Codes of Practice (England and Wales) go to considerable lengths to highlight the importance of good communication, as is shown in Figures 2.1 and 2.2.

2.2 Effective communication is essential in ensuring appropriate care and respect for patients' rights. It is important that the language used is clear and unambiguous and that people giving information check that the information that has been communicated has been understood.

2.3 Everything possible should be done to overcome barriers to effective communication, which may be caused by any of a number of reasons – for example, if the patient's first language is not English. Patients may have difficulty in understanding technical terms and jargon or in maintaining attention for extended periods. They may have a hearing or visual impairment or have difficulty in reading or writing. A patient's cultural background may also be very different from that of the person speaking to them.

2.4 Those with responsibility for the care of patients need to identify how communication difficulties affect each patient individually, so that they can assess the needs of each patient and address them in the most appropriate way. Hospitals and other organisations should make people with specialist expertise (e.g. in sign language or Makaton) available as required.

2.5 Where an interpreter is needed, every effort should be made to identify who is appropriate to the patient, given the patient's gender, religion, language, dialect, cultural background and age. The patient's relatives and friends should only exceptionally be used as intermediaries or interpreters. Interpreters (both professional and nonprofessional) must respect the confidentiality of any personal information they learn about the patient through their involvement.

2.6 Independent advocates engaged by patients can be invaluable in helping patients to understand the questions and information being presented to them and in helping them to communicate their views to staff.

(continued)

(continued)

2.7 Wherever possible, patients should be engaged in the process of reaching decisions which affect their care and treatment under the Act. Consultation with patients involves assisting them in understanding the issue, their role and the roles of others who are involved in taking the decision. Ideally decisions should be agreed with the patient. Where a decision is made that is contrary to the patient's wishes, that decision and the authority for it should be explained to the patient using a form of communication that the patient understands.

Figure 2.1: Communication with patients (Code of Practice (England), Chapter 2).

22.22 Hospital managers must take all practicable steps to ensure the patient understands the areas of information set out in section 132 and 132A of the Act. This does not mean simply telling someone about that information – hospital managers must take such steps as are practicable to ensure that the information has been understood.

22.23 A patient liable to be detained or discharged onto SCT [supervised community treatment] should be given the reasons for detention or community treatment in simple, non-technical language that can be understood and is culturally sensitive, with the reasons including the essential legal and factual grounds for the use of the Act in their particular case.

22.24 Information should be given to the patient both orally and in writing – these are not alternatives. The Welsh Assembly Government has prepared leaflets which can be used as the basis for written information and hospital managers may prepare their own additional documents.

22.25 However, merely repeating what is already written on the information leaflets is inadequate, and those providing information to the patient should give full and clear explanations.

22.26 In line with the guiding principles of this Code, everything possible should be done to overcome any barriers to effective communication. These barriers may be caused by various factors – for example the patient's first language is not English or Welsh or they may not read and write in English or Welsh; they may have difficulty with technical terms and jargon, or maintaining attention for long periods; they may have a hearing or visual impairment or difficulty reading. There may also be barriers to communication associated with the person's mental disorder, for example, the patient may lack mental capacity.

22.27 Members of the multidisciplinary team need to assess and identify how communication difficulties affect each patient individually so that they can address the needs of patients in ways that best suit them. This will need patience and sensitivity. Specialist help should also be made available to staff as required, either from within the hospital, the local social services authority (LSSA) or voluntary organisation. If an intermediary or interpreter is needed, this should not normally be the patient's relative or friend. Staff should make every attempt to find

> *an interpreter appropriate to the patient's needs, bearing in mind the patient's gender, religion, dialect and age. Professional advocates can be invaluable in helping patients understand the questions and information being presented and in helping them communicate their views to staff.*
>
> *22.28 For children, particular consideration should be given to explaining this information in a way they understand and which is sensitive to their needs for emotional reassurance and advice.*

Figure 2.2: How to deliver and explain information (Code of Practice (Wales), Chapter 22).

Case study

Gus Iveson was admitted under section 2 for assessment. He was disorientated and confused. Soon after his admission, Sally, a student nurse who had joined the ward a couple of weeks ago, was told by a senior colleague to go and 'tell him his rights' so that that the task could be recorded as done on the electronic patient record system. They met in a quiet room away from other patients so that they would not be disrupted. Given the way in which the task had been given to her Sally felt under pressure to complete it quickly. Gus found the information difficult to understand. She was impatient to finish and report back to her senior colleague. Gus, however, had a lot of questions about his admission. He also said he was angry with his wife and felt that she had been poisoning him. On learning that he might have to stay in hospital for up to 28 days he became very upset, repeating that his wife had done this to him. Seeing how distressed he was, Sally quickly reflected that her approach had been task- rather than patient-centred. She quickly abandoned her attempt to tell him anything further about his rights and decided instead to listen to his concerns. After talking together for a short while, Gus became more settled and wanted to end the meeting. He said he might feel like talking some more in a while. They agreed to meet later that afternoon when she promised to listen more and, if he was willing, she could tell him some more about his rights.

Detained patients have a number of rights that they are entitled to exercise. The nature of their condition and the circumstances in which they find themselves in hospital may present them with considerable barriers to their being able to exercise their rights.

Having discussed patients' rights and, particularly, the rights of detained patients we end this chapter by looking at some of the points of connection between the MHA and the HRA. In particular we shall look at a number of case law examples which illustrate how the HRA has led to changes to mental health law.

Human rights implications for those detained under the MHA

Remember that the HRA requires that all other legislation (therefore the MHA) is enacted in such a way that it is compatible with the ECHR. If a situation arises where there is a conflict between an existing statute and the HRA then there are ways to address these conflicts.

Ultimately it is for Parliament to decide whether a conflict should be remedied or not. As we have seen, all of the rights contained within the HRA apply to all people, but there are a limited number of rights which seem particularly important to highlight when caring for those who come under the MHA. In this section then we shall discuss some of the Articles which are particularly important for you to keep in view. We shall look at a number of important legal cases which have had an impact on the way in which patients' rights have become better protected.

Article 2: Right to Life

All patients have a right to safe care and treatment which does not place their right to life in jeopardy. One purpose of the MHA is to safeguard a person's right to life where their mental illness may mean that they are a risk to themselves. Generally, where people are detained the 'state' has a *positive obligation* towards those whom it detains to ensure that their rights are protected (which includes safeguarding their right to life). A recent legal case underlined the fact that this positive obligation included those subject to the powers of the MHA.

Case study

Mrs Carole Savage had a history of mental illness and had been treated in hospital on several occasions over a number of years. In 2004 she was detained under section 3. During this admission she absconded from the hospital and committed suicide. Mrs Savage's daughter then brought legal proceedings against the Trust. The basis of her claim was that her mother's right to life had been violated because the Trust did not take proper steps to protect her from the risk that she might kill herself. The Trust argued that because there was no finding of 'gross negligence', Mrs Savage's Article 2 rights had not been breached. The House of Lords eventually found that Mrs Savage's right to life had been breached. The Trust had failed in its operational duty under Article 2 (Savage v. South Essex Partnership NHS Foundation Trust [2008] UKHL 74).

Because Mrs Savage had been detained, the Trust (that is, the state) had a positive 'operational obligation' to protect her from a known risk that she might kill herself. They failed in their duty to take steps which were in the 'scope of their powers' to prevent Mrs Savage from killing herself and Mrs Savage's daughter was awarded damages as a result.

Article 3: Prohibition of Torture or Inhuman or Degrading Treatment or Punishment

Some aspects of care and treatment for mental health patients are undoubtedly contentious (e.g. restraint procedures, the use of seclusion, ECT and neurosurgery) but does this mean that they are inhuman or degrading? The legal case summarised below, although it is now 20 years old, remains important in terms of setting out the grounds on which, for a patient, any treatment would be considered 'inhuman or degrading'. The case highlights, graphically, the very obvious tensions between a duty of care to a patient and lengths which are permissible to go to in order to bring about relief from suffering.

Case study

Mr Herczegfalvy was compulsorily detained in a secure psychiatric hospital in Vienna in the early 1980s. During his detention he was at times force-fed and he was also given medication against his will. To administer both food and medication he was handcuffed and a belt was strapped around his ankles. He was also, at times, secured to a bed. He alleged that because he had been restrained in order to be forcibly given food and medication that he had been subjected to inhuman or degrading treatment contrary to Article 3. The court ruled, however, that there had been no breach of Mr Herczegfalvy's Article 3 rights. This is because where a treatment is a 'therapeutic necessity' then it cannot be either inhuman or degrading. But the court also said that the 'medical necessity' of any treatment would need to be convincingly demonstrated to a court (Herczegfalvy v. Austria [1993] 15 EHRR 437).

What the ruling in this case does *not* mean is that because something is done which is intended, in the minds of those giving the treatment, to be of therapeutic benefit then it will never engage Article 3; it may well do so. The fundamental point is that if there is no convincing evidence base for the treatment *and* it is not done in the patient's best interests then Article 3 will most certainly be engaged.

Article 5: Right to Liberty and Security

This is a limited right meaning that the freedom can be curtailed in certain circumstances. One of these is detention under the MHA. The MHA sets out a proper procedure prescribed by law to deprive someone of their liberty. However, a counterbalancing right is that of the patient to be able to challenge the lawfulness of their detention.

Case study

Until 2001 any patient who was detained under the MHA who chose to appeal against their detention had to prove that they no longer met the criteria for detention to the court (tribunal – see below). The burden of proof rested with the patient to show that they could be discharged rather than with the state (the court) to prove that the grounds for detention continued to be met. But, following a legal case, the Court of Appeal found that section 72 and section 73 of the MHA were incompatible with the HRA. Article 5 (Right to Liberty and Security) of the ECHR places a positive burden on a court (in this case a mental health tribunal) to be satisfied that the grounds on which a person continues to be detained continue to exist. As a result of this case a detailed but significant change to the MHA was made which placed the burden of proof with the state and not with the patient (R(H) v. MHRT North and East London Region [2001] EWCA Civ 415).

However, unless there is what is called a 'proper procedure' in place then any such detention is in breach of Article 5. The unlawful incarceration of a man with autism in hospital led, ultimately, to a change in the law.

Case study

HL had a diagnosis of autism and though he had been an inpatient in the past, he had been living with carers for three years and attended a day centre. He was informally admitted to hospital as, during the course of his attendance at a day centre, his behaviour had deteriorated. He lacked the capacity to consent to treatment and remained in hospital because this was believed to be in his best interests. He was not allowed contact with his carers and was not able to leave. The legal status of HL was questioned; he was not detained under the MHA (at least initially) but neither was he free to leave hospital. At the end of protracted legal proceedings the ECHR ruled that HL had been unlawfully detained. It also ruled that the process of depriving him of his liberty was arbitrary. The net result of this decision was an amendment to the Mental Capacity Act which introduced a new safeguard: the Deprivation of Liberty safeguards (HL v. UK [2004] ECHR 471).

Article 8: Right to Respect for Private and Family Life

This Article has a number of touch points with the MHA because detention cuts across an individual's autonomy. For example, it would include (but is not limited to): visiting rights and restrictions on those visits, privacy and dignity, the use of seclusion, confidentiality and gender separation on wards. As an illustration, the following case study shows how the HRA was used to change the MHA to give patients more of a say in who might act as their 'nearest relative'.

Case study

A woman who was detained under section 3 of the MHA objected to the fact that her adoptive father was the person designated as her nearest relative. She said that he had abused her as a child and was therefore an unsuitable person to have access to any personal information about her (which he would as nearest relative). The woman believed that her rights under Article 8 (Right to Respect for Private and Family Life) had been breached and brought a case (R (M) v. Secretary of State for Health [2003] EWHC 1094 (Admin)). Until then, the MHA provided for the displacement of a nearest relative but patients themselves had no right to challenge the appointment of a nearest relative. As a result of this case section 26 and section 29 of the MHA were declared incompatible with the HRA. It was, however, a further five years before the law was changed and detained patients were given the right to challenge the suitability of a nearest relative to act as such and for the patient to be able to nominate an alternative.

Individuals are entitled to challenge the legality of the MHA, and possible incompatibility with the HRA is one way in which such challenges are brought about. The MHA deprives individuals of some fundamental freedoms and there are, as a consequence, duties placed on those who care for detained patients to ensure that patients know about and are helped to exercise their rights.

Chapter summary

All patients are entitled to respect for their basic human rights. These rights and the values on which they are based make up the building blocks for any consideration of more specific patient rights and entitlements. The HRA and the Equality Act are very important pieces of legislation in protecting the human rights of UK citizens. Following the implementation of the HRA all legislation, including the MHA, should be interpreted so that it does not contradict the protection given to people by the HRA. Sometimes our personal values may interfere with our professional duty to respect the rights of others. Mental health nurses have a professional responsibility to become aware of any particular barriers to respecting patients' rights which may affect the care being given to patients. There are a number of specific rights which mental health nurses must know about in order to provide good quality care to those patients who come under power of the MHA.

Activities: brief outline answers

Activity 2.1

A key issue here relates to the nursing team not understanding their professional duty to inform patients of their rights. A previous error in communicating a patient's rights had failed to bring about practice improvements in the nursing team and they have not been given the opportunity to learn from their mistakes. Incorrect written information is available to patients leading to avoidable misunderstandings and distress. There could be confusion amongst the nursing team around the right of the informal patient to leave the ward which may need to be examined further.

Activity 2.3

Woodbridge and Fulford recorded the following values that people most often gave when they undertook a similar exercise (in no order): honesty, humour, reliability, flexibility, support, caring about others, tolerance, enthusiasm, belonging, fairness, empowering others, socialising, being heard, listening, team working. And here is the list which I came up with (in no order): compassion, justice, honesty, dependability, open-mindedness, respect, acceptance, uniqueness. When comparing your response to those given bear in mind there are no 'right' or 'wrong' answers. Thinking about your values and those that others hold will help you in how you approach situations where conflicting values may be at work. You may wish to repeat this exercise from time to time and see if your list of values changes at all.

Activity 2.5

Although rights are fundamental this does not mean that we can exercise them without restriction. The majority of human rights are limited because for us all to enjoy the freedoms that these rights bring no individual or group can have a greater claim to exercise the right. It is therefore necessary to set limits or conditions on some of the rights so that in exercising a right the rights of others are not ignored or discounted. In exercising our rights we should not infringe the rights of others either wilfully or unintentionally. Ultimately the state has to set limits in order to ensure that all of its citizens are free to exercise their rights. So you will see that, for example, Article 5, the right to liberty and security, is qualified by a number of circumstances, one of which includes the 'lawful detention of ... persons of unsound mind'.

Further reading

Department of Constitutional Affairs (2006) *A Guide to the Human Rights Act,* 3rd edition. London: Department of Constitutional Affairs.

A very clear summary of the HRA which includes an outline of the HRA and the Convention rights.

Department of Health (2007) *Human Rights in Healthcare: A framework for local action.* London: Department of Health.

This guide helps to demystify the subject of human rights and helps to make the links between human rights and healthcare clear. Includes a good number of case examples.

Woodbridge, K and Fulford, KWM (2004) *Whose Values? A workbook for values-based practice in mental health care.* London: Centre for Mental Health.

A very helpful workbook which helps to develop greater understanding of service users and values. It provides tools for mental health nurses to reflect on the way that they work and to recognise the influence that different values have on their practice.

Useful websites

www.cqc.org.uk

The CQC is the regulator for health and social care in England. Publishes an annual monitoring report on the operation of the MHA in England as well as other related documents.

www.dh.gov.uk

This website contains many useful documents relating to the MHA in England including an online copy of the Code of Practice for England stored in its publications' section. You will need to search this site for a copy of the patient information leaflet needed to complete Activity 2.7.

www.gov.uk

Contains many policy and related documents relevant to the NHS.

www.hiw.org.uk

Healthcare Inspectorate Wales is the regulator for health and social care in Wales. Publishes an annual monitoring report on the operation of the MHA in Wales as well as other related documents.

www.legislation.gov.uk

The official home of all UK legislation where you will be able to find copies of all UK Acts of Parliament and related documentation referred to in this book. You will need to search this website to complete Activity 2.5.

www.wales.nhs.uk

This website contains many useful documents relating to the MHA in Wales including a downloadable copy of the Code of Practice for Wales. You will need to search this site for a copy of the patient information leaflet needed to complete Activity 2.7.

Multiple choice questions

1. The Human Rights Act 1998 applies to whom?

   (a) Everyone in the UK
   (b) Everyone in the EU

(c) Everyone except those in prison, and asylum seekers

(d) Everyone except those detained under the Mental Health Act

2. The Equality Act (2006) protects people from discrimination on the grounds of nine 'protected char-acteristics'. Which of these is *not* a protected characteristic?

   (a) Sexual orientation
   (b) Financial means
   (c) Religion or belief
   (d) Disability

3. Patients detained under the Mental Health Act have the right to certain information. Which of these is *not* what they should be told?

   (a) Which of the provisions of the Mental Health Act apply, and their effect
   (b) Their right to appeal
   (c) The way the powers of the Act are monitored
   (d) That they cannot make a complaint

4. The Mental Health Act as far as it allows should be implemented in a way compatible with the European Convention on Human Rights. Because of this, which of the following is false?

   (a) Patients have a right to safe care and treatment which considers their right to life
   (b) It is prohibited for patients to be tortured or suffer inhuman or degrading treatment or punishment
   (c) Patients may not be deprived of their liberty
   (d) Patients have the right to respect for private and family life

Chapter 3
Professional roles and responsibilities

NMC Standards for Pre-registration Nursing Education

This chapter will address the following competencies:

Domain 1: Professional values

5. All nurses must fully understand the nurse's various roles, responsibilities and functions, and adapt their practice to meet the changing needs of people, groups, communities and populations.

7. All nurses must be responsible and accountable for keeping their knowledge and skills up to date through continuing professional development. They must aim to improve their performance and enhance the safety and quality of care through evaluation, supervision and appraisal.

Domain 3: Nursing practice and decision making

9. All nurses must be able to recognise when a person is at risk and in need of extra support and protection and take reasonable steps to protect them from abuse.

9.1. Mental health nurses must use recovery-focused approaches to care in situations that are potentially challenging, such as times of acute distress; when compulsory measures are used; and in forensic mental health settings. They must seek to maximise service user involvement and therapeutic engagement, using interventions that balance the need for safety with positive risk-taking.

Domain 4: Leadership, management and team working

7. All nurses must work effectively across professional and agency boundaries, actively involving and respecting others' contributions to integrated person-centred care. They must know when and how to communicate with and refer to other professionals and agencies in order to respect the choices of service users and others, promoting shared decision making, to deliver positive outcomes and to coordinate smooth, effective transition within and between services and agencies.

NMC Essential Skills Clusters

This chapter will address the following ESCs:

Cluster: Care, compassion and communication

1. As partners in the care process, people can trust a newly registered graduate nurse to provide collaborative care based on the highest standards, knowledge and competence.

By the first progression point
2. Works within limitations of the role and recognises own level of competence.

Cluster: Organisational aspects of care
13. People can trust the newly registered, graduate nurse to promote continuity when their care is to be transferred to another service or person.

By the second progression point
1. Assists in preparing people and carers for transfer and transition through effective dialogue and accurate information.

14. People can trust the newly registered graduate nurse to be an autonomous and confident member of the multi-disciplinary or multi agency team and to inspire confidence in others.

By the second progression point
2. Supports and assists others appropriately.
3. Values others' roles and responsibilities within the team and interacts appropriately.

Chapter aims

By the end of this chapter you will be able to:

- list key tasks which nurses carry out when caring for those subject to compulsion;
- appreciate others' responsibilities and duties under the Act;
- understand how the role of the nurse assists others in carrying out their roles;
- see how changes to the Mental Health Act (MHA) have created new opportunities for nurses to be involved in key decisions about patients' welfare;
- recognise the limitations of the MHA and how good practice depends upon the proper application of the Code of Practice.

Introduction

A noticeable feature of the MHA and its Codes is that they often refer to a number of particular or special roles, individuals or organisations. Many of the roles it refers to are usually carried out by healthcare professionals as part of their wider responsibilities in caring for patients. For example, as a nurse you may one day decide to train to become an approved mental health professional and so would carry out your duties here alongside other work that you would do as a nurse. To care effectively for patients subject to compulsion you will need to be aware of all of the major roles which people have under the MHA. Some of these will be of more direct and immediate relevance to you depending on the type of setting in which you care for those under compulsion.

This chapter is divided into two parts. The first, smaller part summarises the key duties and actions that you may be called upon to carry out as part of your general nursing duties. The second, longer part summarises those activities of certain individuals or organisations which each have specific tasks to fulfil. These are ordered alphabetically. By the end of this chapter you will be familiar with the key tasks and duties of various people along the patient's pathway. As you read through the chapters which follow this, you may find it helpful to refer back to this chapter in order to remind you of the duties of those listed below as you encounter them. In the second part of this chapter then you will find more information about:

- approved clinician (AC);
- approved mental health professional (AMHP);
- hospital manager;
- independent mental health advocate (IMHA);
- Mental Health Act manager;
- mental health tribunal;
- Ministry of Justice (MoJ);
- nearest relative;
- police;
- regulatory authority;
- responsible clinician (RC);
- second opinion appointed doctor (SOAD);
- statutory consultee.

Activity 3.1   *Reflection*

Before working through the remainder of this chapter review the list above. Make brief notes on what you consider to be the main activities, duties or powers of each of those listed. Once done, read through the rest of this chapter reviewing your notes against the text.

As this activity is based on your own knowledge there is no outline answer provided.

Role of the nurse

Caring for those detained under the MHA or those subject to community treatment orders (CTOs) will of course require you to use all of the nursing skills and knowledge that you would draw upon to care for any patient, but there are particular tasks that you may have to undertake as a nurse. As a registered nurse you will have both particular responsibilities under the Act and also be carrying out the requirements of others who have powers under it. For example, you will be responsible for administering authorised leave or 'section 17 leave' which has been granted by the patient's RC. Leave should be permitted following a risk assessment and you have a vital role in evaluating the success of the leave from hospital once a patient has returned. You will also be responsible for initiating procedures to search for someone who has gone missing following a period of leave or who has absconded from hospital. You have, in certain circumstances, the power to prevent someone leaving hospital where you assess that they might present a risk to themselves or others arising from the mental disorder. This is explained more in Chapter 4. As well as administering treatment to those detained under the Act (sometimes without their consent) you may be required to act as a statutory consultee as part of the decision making process around determining whether a particular form of treatment is to be given. You may also be required to receive the detention papers on behalf of the hospital and will therefore need to be satisfied that the detention order is lawful. Where patients choose to appeal against their detention then you may well be asked to prepare a report for an appeal hearing and talk about your report to the panel members. All of these activities are described in more detail either below or in later chapters.

Although much of the care that you provide will be oriented towards promoting recovery and wellbeing, you will also be seeking to protect the welfare of patients as well as prevent harm to others as a result of the risks posed by some patients to others from time to time arising from their mental disorder. Therefore, you will be expected to assist in the management of those who may present risks by, for example, using restraint techniques, using seclusion and carrying out searches on detained patients. The MHA does not provide additional protections or exemptions to you in carrying out these activities; your conduct must always be lawful and in keeping with operational guidelines. Additionally, for these latter three areas, the Codes of Practice provide detailed guidance. It is essential that you receive and follow the training which will be provided to you. All training and guidance should comply with the requirements of the Code.

Case study

A hospital's complaints department received a telephone call from a patient's relative following their visit to see their grandson who had been detained on an acute admission ward two weeks earlier. The patient's grandparents spoke of their concerns about bruising around their grandson's neck; he told them that he had been restrained and that a nurse had 'grabbed him around the throat' whilst he was being held to the ground by several members of staff. The hospital's complaints manager immediately referred the matter on to the hospital's safeguarding lead who, in turn, referred the matter to the local authority safeguarding adults department. The nurse involved was immediately suspended from duty pending a full investigation because of the use of unauthorised and dangerous restraint techniques. The ward's manager was also disciplined for failing to report the matter as a serious untoward incident using the hospital's reporting procedures.

Key roles and responsibilities

Approved clinician

Either a doctor, psychologist, mental health or learning disabilities nurse, occupational therapist or social worker can apply to become an AC on condition that they are also registered with the relevant professional body. An AC is a health or social care professional who has been given special authorisation to carry out various duties under the Act which cannot be carried out by anyone else. Currently approval is given for a period of five years. Only ACs can be in charge of certain treatments and only they can carry out other duties, such as writing court reports on some patients. Many ACs will also be RCs, another role which was introduced following the changes to the MHA (see below).

Approved mental health professional

The duties now carried out by an AMHP were previously carried out by an approved social worker. That role was abolished when the MHA was amended. Now, as well as social workers, an AMHP may be someone who is a registered mental health or learning disability nurse, an occupational therapist or a clinical psychologist. A doctor cannot become an AMHP. Anyone choosing to become an AMHP must be registered with the relevant professional body. Although AMHPs may come from a wider pool of professional backgrounds than before, in practice the vast majority are former approved social workers with relatively few being drawn from those other professional groups.

Most often you will come across an AMHP where someone is being admitted formally under one of the civil powers (see Chapter 5) but they also have an important role in relation to either guardianship or supervised CTOs. One of their core responsibilities is to make their own independent assessment to decide whether to make an application to have someone admitted to hospital compulsorily. An AMHP's assessment differs from that carried out by a doctor in that their role in an assessment is not to diagnose mental disorder but decide whether the use of compulsory powers is the only means by which a person can receive the care and treatment they require. Only if an AMHP is satisfied that detention in hospital is the most appropriate way of providing that care and treatment will they make an application for someone to be detained. Normally an AMHP will require two medical recommendations before they are able to make an application but where someone needs to be admitted in an emergency they can justifiably rely on only one recommendation.

AMHPs also have a range of other interrelated duties related to the application process. These involve formal engagement with someone's nearest relative (NR) and taking or arranging for a person to be taken to hospital once an application has been made. They also have powers in relation to continuing or ending a CTO, returning someone to hospital who has gone absent without leave, and interviewing someone detained by the police under section 136 (see below).

Scenario

Before training as a mental health nurse Haleema Shah had worked as a healthcare assistant in her local mental health hospital, St David's. Since qualifying in 2001 she has worked in two community mental health teams and since 2005 has worked in the assertive outreach team. Following changes to the MHA she decided to train as an AMHP. Initially her colleagues were critical of her decision, believing that she would lose something of her professional identity and that service users would find her dual role difficult to understand. To reassure her colleagues Haleema made a commitment to provide her colleagues with regular updates on her progress at their weekly team meetings and presented a seminar on managing conflicts of interest based on guidance available in the Reference Guide to the Mental Health Act.

Hospital manager

Although in the National Health Service (NHS) we now typically talk of 'executive team member' or 'trust manager' these can be read as synonymous for what the MHA refers to as 'hospital managers'. They are responsible for carrying out a number of functions of the Act but they are not expected to carry these out personally; many will be carried out by others on their behalf. So that the law can be followed correctly, the Code of Practice (para 30.9 (E) 11.8 (W)) requires hospital managers to set out a scheme of delegation which specifies who within the detaining authority has responsibility for carrying out the various functions day to day. Some are rather technical and are not necessary to know in full. However, there are some which are important to be aware of because they are likely to impact on your day to day work with patients. Hospital managers must:

- Make sure that a detention is lawful and that all the necessary procedures have been followed. You are likely to have responsibilities for ensuring that documentation is correct and in order, checking for errors and omissions that could make an application for detention unlawful.
- Give information to detained patients about their rights under the Act. This is typically carried out by both nursing and MHA administration staff working together in the patient's best interests.
- Carry out reviews into detention/supervised community treatment (SCT) and, if, appropriate, exercise their power to discharge someone from detention/SCT. In order to ensure that there is a proper separation of functions hospital managers who hold hearings cannot be employed by the hospital. Typically such panels are comprised of non-executive members of a Trust board and others who are appointed as associate hospital managers specifically for this purpose.
- Hold hospital manager hearings which can take place at any time and may be triggered by the hospital managers or the patient or patient's representative.
- Under the Domestic Violence, Crime and Victims Act 2004 hospital managers are required to inform a victim of crime about a patient's possible discharge or transfer to SCT. The patient will have been detained under Part III (see Chapter 8) and the victim is entitled to make their views known to the hospital about the planned discharge/transfer to SCT. The victim is also entitled to be kept informed about the clinical team's decision making in relation to discharge.

Activity 3.2   *Team working*

During your current or next clinical placement obtain a copy of the scheme of delegation for the operation of the MHA. Identify those tasks which you may be required to carry out as a nurse. At the next available opportunity speak to, and make notes about, your meetings with a range of other staff who have responsibilities under the Act to find out more about how they exercise their roles on behalf of the hospital managers. Share your observations and findings with the ward team.

There is no outline answer for this activity.

Independent mental health advocate

Although advocacy services are a common feature of mental health and learning disability services, IMHAs are specialist advocates that provide advocacy only to patients who are eligible to receive their services (*qualifying patients*); such patients are referred to as qualifying patients. IMHAs therefore do not replace general advocates but provide an additional service to them. Many advocacy service providers also provide IMHA services.

Concept summary: qualifying patients

Section 130C sets who is eligible to receive support from an IMHA. This includes those who are either detained in hospital (including those who are on authorised leave), subject to guardianship or on SCT. Note that people who are detained in hospital under either emergency or holding powers are not eligible. All patients who are considering treatment under section 57 (see Chapter 5) and anyone under 18 who is being considered for electro-convulsive therapy (ECT) are also eligible. It is a legal requirement to tell people who are eligible to receive a service from an IMHA about their right to receive it.

An IMHA must help a patient to understand their rights, and the rights of their nearest relative, which particular parts of the Act apply to them, the planned treatment and the legal framework which governs providing any treatment to them. IMHAs are, by law, given limited access to patients' notes (if a patient has the capacity to consent they can refuse permission).

Case study

Gavin Fletcher had been admitted under section 2 to Dunnett Lodge. Harriet Mathers, a new member of the nursing team, met him for the first time three days after he had been admitted. He had been told about his rights when he first came to the ward and Gavin felt that he didn't want to meet an IMHA so one hadn't been arranged for him. Talking to him about this during her shift Harriet wondered if he might benefit from seeing an IMHA. He had a lot of questions about his treatment and wasn't sure about some of his rights but was reluctant to talk directly to the doctor in charge of his treatment. With Gavin's permission Harriet spoke first to Gavin's doctor and then to the IMHA, Jovinder, who was planning to come to the ward later that afternoon to see another patient. Jovinder met with Gavin in private later that day. They talked about Gavin's treatment plan and she helped him make some notes about what he wanted to say to his doctor. Jovinder agreed to come back later in the week to help him when he had a meeting planned with his RC.

Mental Health Act manager

It is not a statutory requirement to have an MHA manager or administrator to operate within the Act. But, given both the scope and complexity of the Act a hospital will be unable to operate the Act correctly without some specialised, dedicated administrative and legal support. Large mental health trusts typically have an executive level team member who assumes responsibility for the MHA and will also employ an MHA manager as well as a number of MHA administrators. In smaller hospitals, usually in the independent healthcare sector, the role may be carried out on a part-time basis or there may be a service level agreement between hospitals to provide a service. Where such agreements exist the detaining authority retains responsibility for the operation of the Act; they cannot delegate their powers to another authority through any service level agreement. Therefore it is always prudent for any hospital manager to have access to their own independent legal advice aside from any agreement that it may have with a neighbouring hospital to provide administrative support.

Many of the duties that the hospital managers (above) hold are, in practice, delegated to the MHA administration team. Collectively they are responsible for ensuring that the day to day administration of the Act proceeds without incident. The breadth of their responsibilities is wide and will vary from provider to provider depending on its scheme of delegation. Their work will typically include such things as: receiving and scrutinising statutory documentation, arranging to have errors rectified, overseeing transfer orders, giving information to detained patients and their nearest relative and dealing with all aspects of appeal hearings. Other very important services that they offer include training in the operation of the Act, which may be delivered in partnership with clinicians as appropriate and a rolling programme of audit to check that standards are being maintained.

Mental health tribunals

Someone who is detained or subject to community treatment has a right to appeal against their detention. As well as being able to appeal to the hospital managers they can also appeal to a mental health tribunal. Three people make up a tribunal: a lawyer, doctor and a specialist member who will be someone who has relevant experience in the field. The main task of a tribunal is to review detentions at the request of either the patient, their nearest relative, the hospital managers or the Secretary of State for Health (England) or Welsh ministers. There are separate tribunal services for England and Wales. Tribunals are formal hearings where the patient, their legal representative and members of the healthcare team are given an opportunity to say why a detention should or should not continue. As well as hearing arguments the tribunal members will also have read reports which will have been prepared especially for the hearing. Where the hearing is in relation to an inpatient then there is a requirement that a report is prepared and presented by a member of the inpatient nursing team. This can, understandably, be a source of anxiety particularly where attending a tribunal for the first time and therefore it will be extremely important to prepare thoroughly beforehand. Training and support should be available through your employer to assist you. There is also very detailed guidance prepared by the tribunal service itself on its requirements and increasing attention given to this important task within the nursing literature (see Further reading and Chapter 10).

Ministry of Justice

The MoJ has responsibility for two areas of the operation of the MHA in England: the tribunal service (see above) and the 'mental health case work section' which deals with patients subject to restriction orders. In Wales, the MoJ has responsibility for the management of restricted patients only. In summary this department manages, on behalf of the Justice Secretary, the cases of those patients who are subject to restriction orders (see Chapter 8). Because of the risk that such people may pose to the public there are special controls in place. For such patients the MoJ undertakes a case management function so that matters such as permission for leave, transfers between hospitals, discharge and recall to hospital have their oversight.

Nearest relative

The term 'nearest relative' is used in the Act and has a precise meaning, but next of kin, on the other hand, does not. Therefore, again we come across a term which is not used in an everyday conversation because the term has a specific meaning in law. Because a person's nearest relative has a number of rights it is important that there is an unambiguous process in arriving at deciding who a person's nearest relative is. Although, from the patient's point of view, the nearest relative is likely also to be their 'next of kin' a strict hierarchy exists to ensure that there is a reasoned decision making process that is gone through before conferring a set of rights and responsibilities on someone. So, a nearest relative is (in order):

1. husband or wife or civil partner;
2. son or daughter;
3. father or mother;
4. brother or sister;
5. grandparent;
6. grandchild;
7. uncle or aunt;
8. nephew or niece;
9. any other person with whom the patient has ordinarily resided for five years or more.

Because they have a number of important rights, identifying the correct nearest relative is extremely important. You will not be required, as a nurse, ever to need to identify a person's nearest relative; it is the job of the AMHP to do so. However, it is important to be aware of this hierarchy as mistakes can, and do, sometimes occur. This can and does lead to difficulties around the legality of a detention as a result.

A nearest relative can make an application for detention under Part II (see Chapter 4) but this is far from a common occurrence and is discouraged. The AMHP is regarded as the more appropriate person to do so because of their training, but also in order to protect the relationship between the patient and their relative which would no doubt be affected as a result of the detention process. AMHPs have to take proper steps to try to inform or consult a nearest relative about an application. A nearest relative can object to detention under section 3 and so prevent it taking place. A nearest relative can also apply to have someone discharged from hospital but this is not an automatic process and an RC can stop this taking place. Where someone is detained on a section 3 then as a last resort a nearest relative can appeal to a mental health tribunal for the person to be discharged.

There is a counterbalancing power, however, that allows for the removal (displacement) of a nearest relative if such a person is unsuitable and this now includes the right of the patient themselves to apply for displacement. Of course a nearest relative can only exercise their rights if they are made aware of them and we have already seen that there is a statutory duty placed on hospital managers to inform a patient's nearest relative of their rights. In order to try to balance the various rights of different parties the rules about nearest relative are rather technical and complex.

Police

Police officers may be called upon to assist in a number of ways with respect to the care and management of detained patients. The nature of your day to day involvement with the police when caring for detained patients will depend on whether you are caring for patients in hospital or in the community. The police may sometimes assist during an assessment for detention (where there are safety concerns) or assist with the safe return of someone who has gone absent without leave or, lastly, return to detention those who have absconded or escaped from detention.

In addition to these general responsibilities police officers also have two specific powers in relation to those who may be suffering from a mental illness and who require further assessment under the MHA. The first is the power, under section 135, to enter premises in order to remove someone who is considered to be suffering from a mental disorder and who is not receiving appropriate care. This is in order to have the person assessed at a suitable place of safety. This power can only be used when a warrant has been issued by a magistrate. There is a second related power which does not require a warrant for its use by the police. Where someone is believed to be mentally unwell and found in a public place and in need of assessment then the police can, under section 136, detain that person and remove them to a place of safety for the purpose of assessment under the Act. Police officers receive training in the use of these powers and they, along with all others who carry out duties under the Act, need to be attentive to the Code's guiding principles. Even so, naturally enough the involvement of the police, though necessary at times may add to an individual's distress and have unintended negative effects on an individual's vulnerable mental state. Alongside dealing with any immediate action to deal with any crisis or urgent situation you must always be prepared to respond compassionately to the possibility of negative impact that police involvement has had.

Regulatory authority

This is the technical term used in the MHA to refer to the body which is responsible for monitoring operation of the MHA. In England this is currently the Care Quality Commission (CQC).

In Wales the responsibility resides with Welsh ministers but in practice day to day responsibility resides with Healthcare Inspectorate Wales. Only the regulatory authority can:

- monitor the operation of the MHA, report on its findings and require action statements to be produced from its monitoring activity;
- appoint doctors for the purpose of carrying out a second opinion under the Act (SOAD);
- review treatment which has been certified by a SOAD;
- review decisions to withhold correspondence from detained patients.

Although the regulatory authority is responsible for monitoring the MHA and compliance with the Code of Practice, neither the CQC nor Healthcare Inspectorate Wales are responsible for producing it.

Responsible clinician

An RC is an AC (see above) who is in overall charge of a patient's care and treatment. It follows that there can only be one healthcare professional who acts as the RC at any one time. It is the responsibility of hospital managers to make arrangements to ensure that patients have an RC and there should be procedures in place to ensure that this happens. Such procedures should take account, as far as possible, of the patient's views on who the RC should be. Exactly who the RC is will depend on matching the patient's needs to the most suitable AC at any one time and so who acts as RC may well change during the course of a patient's detention. So, given that ACs can be drawn from a range of professions, including nurses, this means that those responsibilities which used to solely be the responsibility of a doctor may now be carried out by professionals other than doctors. For example, if a patient's main treatment needs are medical during an acute phase of an illness then a doctor would act as RC, but for someone whose care needs were centred around recovery, habilitation and rehabilitation then it is possible that a nurse may act as RC. One of the essential requirements in providing effective care is multidisciplinary team working. This is particularly important in the case of detained patients where there is more than one AC involved in providing treatments for a patient. RCs can: renew a period of detention or SCT, discharge a patient from detention or SCT, authorise leave under section 17 and recall someone from leave or SCT.

Second opinion appointed doctor

The MHA makes no reference to the term 'SOAD' as such; it is one of those acronyms which has evolved as a piece of technical shorthand to describe the work that some doctors are asked to carry out from time to time. A SOAD is a doctor, a psychiatrist, who is asked by the regulatory authority, to check that a proposed course of treatment by an AC is suitable and necessary. In practice this means either the CQC (England) or Welsh ministers will each have a panel of suitably qualified psychiatrists who make themselves available to carry out this activity. A SOAD's role is to act as a safeguard to ensure that only appropriate treatment is given to those patients who require it (but who may either not wish to consent or be unable to give their consent). They carry out their work by interviewing the patient, speaking to the person in charge of the patient's treatment and consulting two healthcare professionals who are involved in the patient's care and treatment before reaching their decision. Although the regulatory authority appoints a SOAD for the purpose of the second opinion, the decision made by the SOAD is an independent one: each SOAD is professionally accountable for their actions and there is no right of appeal to the regulatory authority about the SOAD's clinical decision. If a legal challenge were to be mounted by a patient or their representatives then the action would be taken against the individual clinician themselves and not the regulatory authority. Though this may seem like only a minor point of detail, for the patient this distinction is important to keep in view as it should assure the patient that the decision being arrived at by the SOAD is one which is independent of the regulatory authority. However, naturally, as part of its monitoring role the regulatory authority does need to ensure that SOADs work within the operating parameters set by it so that the safeguard does not lose its effectiveness by it not being delivered in a timely way.

Statutory consultee

Before a SOAD is able to issue a certificate to approve the treatment being proposed they must consult two people who are involved in the patient's treatment. You will often find these people referred to as 'statutory consultees'. This isn't a legal term but one which has come into use as a piece of technical shorthand.

There are different rules as to who may fulfil the role of consultee depending on whether the patient is in hospital or on a CTO. If someone is detained then one of the consultees must be a nurse. For those on SCT there is no such requirement. However, in practice, given nurses are highly likely to be involved in someone's care then there is every possibility, once registered, that you will be invited to be involved in this procedure. Should you be asked to act as a consultee you should be able to comment on: the proposed plan of treatment and possible alternatives, the patient's views and wishes about it (as well as those of the patient's carers) and views about the patient's response to treatment which may be given without consent. Both Codes (England 24.49–24.54; Wales 18.19–18.23) give detailed guidance on this important safeguard which should be referred to. You can decline to act as a consultee should you believe that you are not able to fulfil the role.

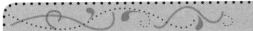

Chapter summary

In this chapter you have been introduced to a number of individuals and organisations which each have powers and responsibilities under the Act. The key responsibilities of each have been given and you have been made aware of the way in which nurses are uniquely placed to carry out some of these responsibilities or to assist others so that the various tasks can be accomplished. As a result you should now be more able to help patients more effectively by advocating on their behalf where you recognise that errors in the administration of the law have occurred, by involving other members of the multidisciplinary team as appropriate and practising safely by knowing with greater certainty the scope and limitations of the law.

Further reading

Brown, R (2013) *The Approved Mental Health Professional's Guide to Mental Health Law*, 3rd edition. London: Sage/Learning Matters.

This is a concise practitioner guide to how the AMHP role interacts with the MHA and the Mental Capacity Act.

Department of Health (2008) *Reference Guide to the Mental Health Act 1983.* London: TSO.

This is the best guide to the roles and responsibilities of each professional involved in MHA assessments. Though not statute law it functions as guidance which professionals are expected to follow or give good reason and rationale for not doing so.

Hewitt, D (2009) *Nearest Relative Handbook*, 2nd edition. London: Jessica Kingsley.

This handbook details the complicated legal issues around the definition of powers, declaration and displacement of the nearest relative and has been updated to include the amended MHA 2007.

Jones, R (2012) *Mental Health Act Manual.* London: Sweet & Maxwell.

Richard Jones's *Mental Health Act Manual* has long been a standard reference for approved social workers and now AMHPs. It details statute law and guidance with detailed notes and reference to case law.

National Institute for Mental Health in England (2008) *Mental Health Act 2007: New roles.* London: Department of Health.

The Mental Health Act 2007 allows a broader range of professionals to carry out a range of functions under the Act. This guidance focuses on the new roles of approved mental health professional, approved clinician and responsible clinician.

Useful websites

http://www.justice.gov.uk/tribunals/mental-health

For information on the tribunal service including guidance on preparing to attend a hearing.

Multiple choice questions

1. Which of the following *cannot* be an approved clinician?

    (a) Doctor or psychologist
    (b) Mental health or learning disability nurse
    (c) Healthcare assistant or domestic worker
    (d) Occupational therapist or social worker

2. When deciding who is a patient's nearest relative, which comes after husband or wife or civil partner, son or daughter, father or mother?

    (a) Uncle or aunt
    (b) Grandparent
    (c) Brother or sister
    (d) Grandchild

3. Which of the following duties apply to the regulatory authority?

   (a) Appoint doctors for the purpose of carrying out a second opinion under the Act (SOAD)
   (b) Write and review the code of practice
   (c) Appoint responsible clinicians for hospitals
   (d) Assess patients for the purpose of detaining them

4. What is the name given to the approved clinician in overall charge of a patient's care and treatment?

   (a) Responsible clinician
   (b) Second opinion appointed doctor
   (c) Mental Health Act manager
   (d) Independent mental health advocate

Chapter 4
Admission and detention in hospital

By the third progression point

9. Ensures access to independent advocacy.

10. Recognises situations and acts appropriately when a person's choice may compromise their safety or the safety of others.

Cluster: Organisational aspects of care

10. People can trust the newly registered graduate nurse to deliver nursing interventions and evaluate their effectiveness against the agreed assessment and care plan.

By the second progression point

5. Detects, records, reports and responds appropriately to signs of deterioration or improvements, communicating changes to colleagues.

18. People can trust a newly registered graduate nurse to enhance the safety of service users and identify and actively manage risk and uncertainty in relation to people, the environment, self and others.

By the first progression point

5. Under supervision works within legal frameworks to protect self and others.

By the second progression point

7. Contributes to promote safety and positive risk taking.

Entry to the register

11. Assesses and implements measures to manage, reduce or remove risk that could be detrimental to people, self and others.

Chapter aims

By the end of this chapter you will be able to:

- describe the difference between informal and compulsory admission to hospital;
- show awareness of the criteria for different types of civil detention in hospital;
- identify the principal rights that detained patients have;
- understand when and how emergency holding powers might be used by nursing or other professionals.

Introduction

In this chapter we look at the main sections of the Mental Health Act (MHA) which are concerned with people with a mental disorder being admitted to hospital compulsorily, that is, detained against their will. There are two principal routes (either through use of civil powers or through the courts) by which an individual can be detained. Here we discuss the civil routes and in Chapter 8 we examine the role of the courts and police. We will describe the key characteristics of each of the civil detention sections and the relevant procedures for detention. We emphasise the particular duties that you have towards detained patients and also your specific powers under section 5(4). The majority of people admitted to mental health hospitals are known as *informal* or *voluntary* patients and so to begin with we shall take a closer look at this group of patients.

Informal (voluntary) admission to hospital

Not everyone who has a mental health problem either can be, or ought to be, detained in hospital to receive care and treatment compulsorily for their mental illness. Surveys have estimated that almost one person in four suffers with a mental health problem each year in England (Singleton et al., 2001). The overwhelming majority of these receive care and treatment provided by either primary or secondary healthcare services without them needing to go into hospital.

Patients in mental health hospitals who are not detained are commonly referred to as informal patients (s131). Strictly speaking, someone receiving care and treatment in a hospital who is not detained could either be a 'voluntary' or an 'informal' patient. A voluntary patient is in hospital because they have given their consent to be admitted and agree to remain and receive care and treatment. An informal patient does not have the capacity to make a decision about whether they need to be in hospital but they do not resist being admitted to or remaining in hospital. Sometimes, because of the way in which a person may be affected by their mental illness, they may move between being a voluntary patient to an informal patient and vice versa. Note that the Codes of Practice (England p366; Wales p226) do not in fact distinguish between these two groups and use the term 'informal' to apply to both.

Case study

Fiona Dalgetty, 42 and recently separated from her husband, was admitted to Joshua Ward, St Peter's Hospital just over three weeks ago in a hypomanic state. Before her admission she had been receiving care from the crisis resolution team for a number of weeks. Detained under the MHA (status: formal or detained) her condition improved quickly over the course of her first week in hospital. Towards the end of the second week, following a meeting with her responsible clinician (RC) and other members of the multi-disciplinary team (MDT), the medication that she had been prescribed and given (sometimes against her wishes) was reduced and she agreed to continue to take it. She recognised that she had been unwell and acknowledged that she had been behaving out of character for several months. Following a further review some days afterwards, her RC then decided it was no longer necessary for her to be detained. Fiona understood why she was in hospital and agreed to stay (status: voluntary patient). During the course of the following week, however, her mood lowered considerably. Her thinking slowed and she had difficulty concentrating. She could no longer say why she needed to be in hospital. She became increasingly passive and made no attempt to participate in any of the ward's activities, preferring instead to sit quietly in the interfaith room (status: informal patient). Although nursing staff tried to persuade her to continue to take her medication she declined it on a number of occasions. At this point her RC and the MDT reviewed her again to decide whether she should be considered for detention once again.

This case study illustrates the difference between someone who is able to make an active decision to stay in hospital and someone who is not. We see how a person's capacity to make such a decision can change depending on how their mental health is affected by their experience of mental illness.

Concept summary: what does capacity mean?

The Mental Capacity Act (MCA) 2005 rather than the MHA is the statute which helps us understand the legal concept of capacity. It is concerned with making decisions on behalf of anyone over the age of 16 who is unable (mentally incapable) to make a decision about something for themselves. The MCA enshrines in law five principles that underpin the statute. These are:

- *A person must be assumed to have capacity unless it is established that he lacks capacity.*
- *A person is not to be treated as unable to make a decision unless all practicable steps to help him to do so have been taken without success.*
- *A person is not to be treated as unable to make a decision merely because he makes an unwise decision.*
- *An act done, or decision made, under this Act for or on behalf of a person who lacks capacity must be done, or made, in his best interests.*
- *Before the act is done, or the decision is made, regard must be had to whether the purpose for which it is needed can be as effectively achieved in a way that is less restrictive of the person's rights and freedom of action.*

(MCA, s1)

And a person is defined as lacking capacity where:

in relation to a matter if at the material time he is unable to make a decision for himself in relation to the matter because of an impairment of, or a disturbance in the functioning of, the mind or brain.

(MCA, s2(1))

The MCA (s3) also sets out four factors which must be taken into account when deciding whether a person has capacity to make a particular decision. Someone lacks the capacity to make a decision if they are unable to:

- understand the information relevant to the decision;
- retain that information;
- use or weigh that information as part of the process of making the decision;
- communicate their decision.

A judgement about a person's capacity is bound up with an assumption that a person has capacity to make a decision until it can be shown that this is not the case by assessing it.

The rights of informal patients

As a nurse you are bound by your general duty of care to protect the rights of all patients irrespective of their status under the MHA. But because the MHA is concerned with detained patients it does not, as a general rule, concern itself with the rights of informal patients. There are other statutes and guidance which apply (see Chapter 2). There are some limited exceptions to this, however, concerning the safeguards around consent to treatment (Chapter 5). Likewise therefore the Codes of Practice are also limited in their discussion of the rights of informal patients.

Activity 4.1   *Reflection*

The Codes of Practice state: *Although the Act does not impose any duties to give information to informal patients, these patients should be made aware of their legal position and rights (E 2.45/ W22.37).*

Summarise what you understand to be some of the main rights that informal patients have. In considering your answer refer to the case study above as well as Chapter 2.

There is an outline answer at the end of the chapter.

Detention under the MHA

Anyone who is detained under the MHA must, first of all, be suffering from a mental disorder. Second, this mental disorder must then be judged as affecting them in ways which mean that it is necessary for them to be admitted. When these facts have been established one of several powers may be used to detain someone in hospital. This section summarises each of the four different civil powers. As you read through the various sections you will see that each is designed to be used in certain circumstances. The decision to use one power instead of another, or no power at all, rests with the professionals charged with making those decisions. They will be guided by a range of factors including the statutory requirements themselves, guidance from the Code of Practice, case law, their professional training and accepted clinical or professional practice.

Your duty of care towards people compulsorily admitted to hospital

The nurse's role is primarily derived from her statutory responsibility to practise within the Nursing and Midwifery Council's (NMC's) *Code of Conduct* (2008). Founded on the principle of trust, the Code states:

The people in your care must be able to trust you with their health and wellbeing. To justify that trust, you must:

- *make the care of people your first concern, treating them as individuals and respecting their dignity*
- *work with others to protect and promote the health and wellbeing of those in your care, their families and carers, and the wider community*
- *provide a high standard of practice and care at all times*
- *be open and honest, act with integrity and uphold the reputation of your profession*

(NMC, 2008, p2)

In addition, as we have seen in Chapter 1, the Code of Practice sets out five guiding principles which need to be considered by anyone who is making a decision in relation to the MHA. There are two major implications which follow.

First, as a nurse you will be in a unique and privileged position as the member of the MDT most closely involved in the day to day care of patients on the ward. Your nursing assessments will be critical contributions to the formulation and implementation of an appropriate plan of care for all your patients. Your ability to observe, and communicate your observations accurately, are also vitally important in contributing to the work of others who have specific roles and responsibilities under the Act. Without a sound awareness of the powers and duties that the Act confers on all those who work within its provisions you will not be able to fulfil your statutory obligations as an accountable practitioner.

Second, flowing from the principle of working with others to protect and promote health, nurses also have an important advocacy role. Those who are disempowered because they have been detained will often need special help to ensure that their rights are safeguarded, their dignity respected and their health and wellbeing protected. Based on her knowledge of the patient and in accordance with her duty set out in the NMC's Code, the nurse is uniquely placed to ensure that the particular wishes and needs of the patient are communicated to other members of the care team. All professionals involved in the process of detention have to demonstrate that detention (and therefore only detention) is necessary in order to provide the care and treatment that a person needs. Unless the needs and wishes of the patient are known then the fullest consideration of possible alternatives to detention will not have been made.

Defining mental disorder

The MHA does not have a great deal to say about particular forms or types of mental disorder. In Part I of the Act we see that, as far as the law is concerned, mental disorder is very broadly defined as *any disorder or disability of the mind* (s1(2)). But there are two important qualifications that the nurse needs to be aware of.

The first is that section 1 makes clear that dependence on drugs or alcohol is not to be considered as a form of mental disorder. No one can be detained in hospital for treatment of such an addiction alone. But if an individual has a mental disorder which satisfies the criteria for detention as well as an addiction to drugs or alcohol then they may come within the scope of the provisions of the Act (if other conditions are met, which we discuss below).

The second concerns people with a learning disability. A learning disability is defined as being a *state of arrested or incomplete development of the mind which includes significant impairment of intelligence and social functioning* (s1(4)). People with a learning disability can be detained in hospital because the Act views it as a mental disorder. But unless the nurse is working in a specialised service for those with learning disabilities she is unlikely to encounter many who are detained. This is because it is only when an individual's learning disability is also *associated with abnormally aggressive or seriously irresponsible conduct* (s1(2A)) that they can be detained on a longer term basis. Naturally there are instances where someone with a learning disability is detained in hospital as a result of a co-existing mental disorder.

Activity 4.2   *Reflection*

In a group, think through and discuss your reactions to the use of the terms 'mental disorder' 'mentally disordered' and 'patient' as used in the Act and Code of Practice. How do these terms differ from others that you have come across in your training? When might they be helpful and when might they hinder you in caring for people detained in hospital?

There is no outline answer to this activity.

Activity 4.3   *Critical thinking*

Why do you think the MHA does not offer a more detailed definition of mental disorder, which may include the types or forms of mental disorder that the Act is concerned with?

An outline answer is given at the end of the chapter.

The numbers of people admitted compulsorily to hospital

We have already stated that many patients admitted to hospital are not detained under the MHA but a large minority are. The National Health Service (NHS) Information Centre produces statistics each year derived from data supplied to it through a national data collection exercise (the Mental Health Minimum Dataset). Their 2011 report for the period 2009/2010 showed that:

- there is a small downward trend in the total numbers of people being admitted to hospital for treatment for a mental disorder over the past five years;
- there has been an increase in the numbers of detained patients in the corresponding period. From being just over 25 per cent of the total in 2005/6 they accounted for almost 40 per cent of the total in 2009/10.

	Not detained		Formally detained					All inpatients
	total	%	Place of safety	Part II	Court and prison dispersals	total	%	
2005/06	82,913	74.6	457	25,603	2,115	28,175	25.4	111,088
2006/07	78,367	73.5	501	25,795	1,898	28,194	26.5	106,561
2007/08	73,165	69.2	857	29,465	2,232	32,554	30.8	105,719
2008/09	69,922	68.2	910	29,362	2,377	32,649	31.8	102,571
2009/10	65,286	60.6	1,461	37,249	3,769	42,479	39.4	107,765

Table 4.1: Percentage of inpatients detained in hospital, by year.

Source: Mental Health Bulletin, Fourth report from Mental Health Minimum Dataset (MHMDS) annual returns, 2010. © 2011, The Health and Social Care Information Centre.

Though the majority of mental health inpatients are still admitted informally, there are a growing number of people who are formally detained. So, not only is it increasingly likely that you will care for detained patients in an inpatient setting, it is also the case, as we shall see in Chapter 7, that nurses working in community settings will also care for patients who are subject to the use of the Act through the use of community treatment orders.

Part I of the Act, discussed above, dealt with defining mental disorder. Part II is concerned with the formal admission (detention) in hospital of someone from the community or who is already in hospital. There are four different sections under which a person may be detained depending upon the circumstances in each case (sections 2, 3, 4 or 5). We have already seen that anyone being assessed for detention under the Act must be suffering from a mental disorder. But, it is only when someone has been further assessed as meeting other criteria that formal detention can proceed.

The conditions which need to be met are different in each of the sections because they are intended to be used in different circumstances. We look at these next.

Activity 4.4 — *Critical thinking*

To care for patients well you will need to be familiar with different types of detention and their implications for the patient. To familiarise yourself with the different criteria take a look at some of the blank statutory forms relating to admission under Part II of the Act (in England these are forms A1–A11; in Wales forms HO1–HO11) (see Useful websites at the end of this chapter). What do you notice about the forms in terms of their wording, structure and layout? You may find it helpful to refer to your notes and copies of the forms as you work through the rest of this chapter.

An outline answer is given at the end of the chapter.

Section 2 (admission for assessment)

> ### Case study
>
> *Trenton Hurst was taken to Hamilton Hospital by the police at 5.45 a.m. one Wednesday morning. A little earlier, a motorist had seen him walking, partly dressed and barefooted down the exit slip road of a dual carriageway. Stopping his car the motorist phoned the police and then went to Trenton's aid. Speaking only in a barely audible whisper Trenton could give no clear account why he had been walking towards oncoming traffic, saying only that he felt tired. He appeared frightened and bewildered. There was no evidence that he had been drinking and no sign of any injury. So, concerned for his welfare, the police decided that he needed to be further assessed and took him, using their power under section 136 to a place of safety at the hospital (see Chapter 8 for discussion of police powers).*
>
> *At the hospital he was supported by a nurse and the police waited with him until another team of people arrived to carry out an assessment. The assessing team found out that he had been signed off work for some time following the sudden death of his twin brother in a road traffic accident. Trenton also told them that he used cannabis occasionally but that he did not use other drugs habitually. He had been receiving treatment with anti-depressants for four weeks. Given the circumstances in which he had been found, his recent history of ill health, his inability to account for his actions coherently, his preoccupied manner and dishevelled state it was felt that that he posed a continuing considerable risk to his own health and safety if he was allowed to leave hospital. The approved mental health professional (AMHP) decided that a period of assessment in hospital was needed and he made an application under section 2 which was supported by the two medical recommendations provided by the doctors who were part of the team.*

Someone detained for assessment of their mental disorder under section 2 can be detained in hospital for up to 28 days, but they may be transferred to another detention order or discharged from this order any time during this period. An assessment order cannot be renewed when the time limit has been reached. Under this section some forms of treatment may be administered without a patient's consent. You must, however, ensure that you uphold your professional duty to work sensitively and co-operatively with patients so that the likelihood of administering treatment against their wishes is reduced as far as possible. As the case study above illustrates, this section is intended to be used in those circumstances where a number of factors are unknown about the patient's condition. Both Codes of Practice give guidance (England 4.26; Wales 5.2) as to when an application under section 2 should be made. Although the precise wording in the two Codes differs the key points are that this section should be used when:

- *the full extent of the nature and degree of a patient's condition is unclear;*
- *there is a need to carry out an initial in-patient assessment in order to formulate a treatment plan, or to reach a judgement about whether the patient will accept treatment on a voluntary basis following admission; or*

- *there is a need to carry out a new in-patient assessment in order to re-formulate a treatment plan, or to reach a judgement about whether the patient will accept treatment on a voluntary basis.* (England 4.26)

In our example, all of the facts about Trenton's condition were not fully known. Although he had been previously diagnosed as suffering from depression by his general practitioner (GP) it did not appear to the assessment team that depression was the only possible explanation which would account for his present confused state.

Three people are involved in the decision to detain someone under this section: an AMHP (or the individual's nearest relative) and two doctors. Each has particular responsibilities and tasks to complete.

The approved mental health professional's role

The AMHP's job is to decide whether an application to detain someone should be made. In deciding this, the AMHP must judge whether, taking into account all the circumstances, he is satisfied that detention is the most appropriate way of providing the care and treatment that the individual needs. You will have noticed from your review of the statutory forms that the AMHP must declare that they have interviewed the patient themselves to make this judgement. In making his decision the AMHP considers the recommendations made by the two doctors. Section 11(3) also requires the AMHP to take reasonable steps to inform the patient's nearest relative of the fact that an application either is about to be made, or already has been made.

The doctors' role

Two doctors each give an opinion which states that a period of assessment in hospital is necessary. Without these two recommendations an application cannot go ahead. You will have noticed from your review of the statutory forms (Form A3/A4 or HO3/HO4) that the doctor is required to state whether or not they are approved under section 12. This is because one of the recommendations must be made by a doctor who has 'special experience in the diagnosis or treatment of mental disorder'. It is also usual for one or other of the doctors to have had previous acquaintance with the individual before they examined them for the purposes of making a recommendation. The Codes of Practice (England 4.73; Wales 2.58) state that whilst it is preferable that this *should be a doctor who has personally treated the patient [Wales: 'knows the patient professionally'] … it is sufficient for the doctor to have had some previous knowledge of the patient's case.* Each doctor's examination is to see whether the person meets the criteria for detention under section 2 which are:

- *that the individual is suffering from mental disorder of a nature or degree which warrants the detention of the patient in a hospital for assessment (or for assessment followed by medical treatment) for at least a limited period; and*
- *he ought to be so detained in the interests of his own health or safety or with a view to the protection of other persons.*

The nearest relative's role

Although the law allows for an individual's nearest relative to make an application (Form A1/HO1) the practice is discouraged. The reasons why are set out in the Code (para. 4.28–4.30) and are to do with the AMHPs suitability because of their professional training and the need to avoid a negative impact on the relationship between the patient and nearest relative were a nearest relative to make an application. A nearest relative does have the right to request that an AMHP (through the local social services authority) considers whether an application ought to be made (s13(4)).

Patient's rights

Patients have a right to appeal against their detention within the first 14 days and the right to receive help from an independent mental health advocate. Nurses have an extremely important role in helping patients to understand and exercise their rights. The Department of Health in England and NHS Wales produce patient information leaflets for this and other sections (see list of Useful websites).

Section 3 (admission for treatment)

Someone may be detained for treatment under this section initially for a period of up to six months. Unlike section 2, the order can be renewed, in the first instance for a further six months and then, if necessary, at yearly intervals afterwards.

The Code of Practice (E) states that section 3 should be used if:

- *the patient is already detained under section 2 (because detention under section 2 cannot be renewed by a new section 2 application); or*
- *the nature and current degree of the patient's mental disorder, the essential elements of the treatment plan to be followed and the likelihood of the patient accepting treatment on a voluntary basis are already established.*
(para. 4.27)

The intention here is that this order should be considered where there is a clear view that a person is in need of treatment for their mental disorder and they are unlikely to agree to receive that treatment unless they are detained.

Case study

Stuart Robinson had been receiving support from the local intensive home treatment team for the past two weeks in order to prevent a further deterioration in his mental health. He had become gradually more unkempt in his appearance and stopped attending a local group run by Rethink. He had been diagnosed as suffering from schizophrenia seven years ago and had had a number of admissions to hospital. Initially he had seemed accepting of the offer of help from the care team and allowed them entry to his home.

Despite being visited frequently by one of the team's members his ability to care for himself showed no sign of improvement. He grew increasingly suspicious of some members of the team, missed a number of the appointments and did not respond to telephone calls. Towards the end of the second week of the team's involvement, Stuart's sister telephoned the team leader. A neighbour had complained to her that Stuart had been seen in the garden early that morning dressed only in a vest. He had been described as standing motionless for long periods of time, staring at the wall, sometimes urinating in a corner of the yard and scooping up handfuls of water direct from the garden's water butt. An urgent review meeting was held and a decision made that a further assessment was necessary to establish if Stuart needed admission to hospital for treatment. Stuart was admitted later that day under section 3 of the MHA.

An AMPH makes an application in a similar way to that for section 2. However, there is an additional duty placed on the AMHP to consult rather than simply inform the individual's nearest relative. In this case a nearest relative may object to a detention order being made and if so the detention cannot be made (s11(4)). This right is counterbalanced by another provision (s29) which means that a nearest relative can be prevented from exercising this power if their objection to an application appears unreasonable. However, this takes time as it involves an application by the AMHP to the county court (and there is no guarantee that the court will agree with the application).

Compared to section 2 there are some important differences in the detail of the opinions that the doctors are asked to give (MHA, s3(2)). When making their recommendations the doctors are, in effect, stating that they believe that there are clearer grounds for admitting someone compulsorily for treatment because there is less doubt about the individual's condition and their likely response to being offered treatment. There is also a requirement on them to state that appropriate medical treatment for the patient's mental disorder is available at a specified hospital, group of hospitals or within a particular part of a hospital.

As with section 2 the patient has a number of rights including the right to appeal against their detention at any time and the right to meet an independent mental health advocate. A patient may only leave hospital if leave has been authorised by the RC in charge of their treatment (this is also true for those detained under s2). Once a patient has received treatment for three months they must be asked for their consent for the treatment to continue. If they do not wish to, or are unable to consent, then treatment has to be authorised by a second opinion appointed doctor (SOAD). This is commonly known as the 'three month rule' and the time period begins from when the patient first started to receive treatment for their mental disorder (and not the date on which they were admitted; see Chapter 5 Medical treatment).

Section 4 (admission for assessment in cases of emergency)

This power is used when, if it were not for the urgent need to admit someone to hospital, a section 2 order would be used. A person can be detained for up 72 hours and it is only to be used in situations where there is a *genuine emergency* (Code of Practice, para. 5.4). An application by an

AMHP is accompanied by only one medical recommendation. A key issue here is that only one doctor is available to assess the patient. The AMHP, in making the application, must state that, in their opinion, it would be undesirable to delay admitting someone by having to follow the requirements for an application under section 2. Your review of Form A11/HO11 will have shown you that the grounds for recommending admission are identical to those for section 2 (Form A3/HO3 or A4/HO4) with the important addition that it is of 'urgent necessity' for the patient to be admitted to hospital.

An individual has a right of appeal against their detention as they would for section 2. The laws that govern medical treatment of informal patients (see Chapter 5) are the ones which apply to patients detained under section 4, that is, a person must not be treated for their mental disorder without their consent. If, however, a second medical recommendation is received within the 72 hours then a section 4 order becomes a section 2 order (starting from the time that the s4 order commenced). Although authorised (s17) leave could be granted, in practice, given the emergency nature of the admission, any authorisation by the RC will be weighed very closely against risk factors.

Section 5 (application in respect of a patient already in hospital)

The powers in this section allow an application for detention to be made even though a patient is already in hospital. It may also be used to stop an informal patient from leaving hospital until an assessment for detention has been carried out. There are two types of 'holding powers' (England Code of Practice Ch12; Wales Code of Practice Ch8). Section 5(2) is often referred to as 'the doctor's holding power' though it can be invoked by either a doctor or an approved clinician (see Chapter 3). A patient can be prevented from leaving hospital for up to 72 hours if the doctor or approved clinician is of the view that an individual should be detained under section 2 or section 3. The period of detention begins when a report has been submitted to the hospital's managers setting out the reasons why an application for detention should be made.

Section 5(4) deals with 'the nurse's holding power' which is of a much shorter duration, up to six hours. In this instance a nurse of what the Act refers to as the 'prescribed class' (a registered mental health or learning disability nurse) may prevent an informal patient from leaving hospital if certain conditions are met. It is intended only to be used in emergencies and when a doctor or approved clinician who may institute section 5(2) is not immediately available. Once used, it cannot be extended or renewed and it only applies where a patient is in hospital receiving treatment for their mental disorder. In using this power the nurse makes a declaration that:

- *it appears to them that the patient is suffering from mental disorder to such a degree that it is necessary for his health or safety or for the protection of others for him to be immediately restrained from leaving the hospital; and*
- *it is not practicable to secure the immediate attendance of a practitioner [or clinician] for the purpose of furnishing a report under subsection (2) above.*

The Codes of Practice offer some very helpful guidance around the use of this power. The Code for England sets this out as follows:

12.27 Before using the power, nurses should assess:

- *the likely arrival time of the doctor or approved clinician, as against the likely intention of the patient to leave. It may be possible to persuade the patient to wait until a doctor or approved clinician arrives to discuss the matter further; and*
- *the consequences of a patient leaving the hospital before the doctor or approved clinician arrives – in other words, the harm that might occur to the patient or others.*

12.28 In doing so, nurses should consider:

- *the patient's expressed intentions;*
- *the likelihood of the patient harming themselves or others;*
- *the likelihood of the patient behaving violently;*
- *any evidence of disordered thinking;*
- *the patient's current behaviour and, in particular, any changes in their usual behaviour;*
- *whether the patient has recently received messages from relatives or friends; whether the date is one of special significance for the patient (e.g. the anniversary of a bereavement);*
- *any recent disturbances on the ward;*
- *any relevant involvement of other patients;*
- *any history of unpredictability or impulsiveness;*
- *any formal risk assessments which have been undertaken (specifically looking at previous behaviour); and*
- *any other relevant information from other members of the multi-disciplinary team.*

12.29 Nurses should be particularly alert to cases where patients suddenly decide to leave or become determined to do so urgently.

12.30 Nurses should make as full an assessment as possible in the circumstances before using the power, but sometimes it may be necessary to invoke the power on the basis of only a brief assessment.

Again, minor variations occur between the two Codes in terms of language and style but essentially each deals with the same factors and contingencies (England 12.28–12.30; Wales 8.22–8.25).

Case study

Jo Bishop had been Fiona Delgatty's named nurse since her admission to Joshua Ward three weeks earlier. Having first been admitted under section 2 Fiona then agreed to stay on the ward informally. She had been declining medication over the past few days. Though often saying little, Fiona had started to talk more recently, in terms of the hopelessness of her situation, how she felt she had failed and that it

(continued)

continued ...

> was probably right for her to be in hospital as she needed to be taught a lesson. A full multidisciplinary review team meeting was planned for the next day. Towards the end of the evening, Fiona received a phone call from her estranged husband, the first since her admission. Soon afterwards, she approached Jo in a distressed state saying that she wanted to leave the hospital immediately, that she felt fine and that she realised that being in hospital wasn't going to be of any help. Her decision struck Jo as very concerning because it was so impulsive. Given the sudden change in her intentions Jo asked if she could spend time talking with Fiona to understand why it had become so urgent that she leave. Jo's view was that it would be better for Fiona to stay on the ward at least until the MDT meeting had taken place so that her wish to discharge herself could be discussed then. Eventually Fiona reluctantly agreed to stay on the ward but only until she could be seen by a doctor that evening. A doctor was available, but not for another hour. Jo discussed her concerns and the plan with other members of the nursing team before going for her rest break. Whilst Jo was off the ward Fiona walked hurriedly towards the entrance door with her belongings in her bag. Jo's colleague, Wes, stopped Fiona from leaving the ward and reported his actions to the hospital's senior manager on duty immediately.

If section 5(4) is in place when a section 5(2) is invoked, the section 5(2) is deemed to have started when the section 5(4) began. So, the maximum amount of time that a patient can be held on this section is 72 hours. A patient held under section 5(2) or (4) has no right of appeal and cannot be treated without their consent. If the patient is not detained under either section 2 or section 3 then the holding power lapses and the patient becomes an informal patient.

Making sure detentions are lawful

Case study

Jennie Walters had recently qualified and had been appointed to work on one of the acute care wards at her local hospital. As part of her induction she had received some training on the MHA from the hospital's mental health act manager. She learned about the hospital's policy and procedure for receiving and scrutinising the statutory forms (detention papers) completed by the AMHP and doctors when someone was admitted to the ward. During her training she had learned that some mistakes on the forms could easily be put right but others were more serious and could mean that the person's detention might not be lawful. The mental health act manager taught her about the hospital's detention documents checklist. She was told that it was the job of the nurse in charge of the ward to go through this when admitting the patient to the ward. The AMHP would usually be expected to be available to go through forms with the nurse in charge. The checklist also gave clear instructions to follow if any mistakes were found during the checking process.

All hospitals which detain patients ought to have formal arrangements in place to check that a patient is lawfully detained. A scheme of delegation should set out who specifically is authorised to carry out the various duties that hospital managers have. At the point of admission, one task is to check that the documents authorising detention are sound. All hospitals will have their own policy and procedures to ensure that their scrutiny processes comply with section 15 (Rectification of applications and recommendations). Only when you have received further training would you be expected to undertake detailed scrutiny of documentation and to distinguish between different types of error and their significance. Some errors, for example, are rectifiable within a given time frame (14 days) and others are not so serious that failure to put them right would make the application invalid. However, as you may well be required to receive documents on behalf of the hospital at the point of admission it is important to understand that some errors are so serious that they make the application unlawful and the only remedy is to start afresh. The *Reference Guide to the Mental Health Act 1983* (England) gives some examples where the documents cannot be regarded as proper, for example:

- *the application is not accompanied by the correct number of medical recommendations*
- *the application and the recommendations do not all relate to the same patient*
- *the application or recommendation is not signed at all, or is signed by someone not qualified to do so*
- *the application does not specify the correct hospital.*

(para. 2.91)

Chapter summary

Reviewing this chapter you will have picked up a number of key facts about how certain people with mental health problems can be detained so that they can receive the care and treatment that they would otherwise not get. You have been given an outline of the process of detention for sections 2, 3, 4 and 5. You will also now be familiar with some of the powers of the Act, for example the restrictions on rights to leave hospital and the power to give some treatments in certain circumstances without an individual's consent. You have been made aware of the particular rights that people have who are detained. You have also been shown the importance that the NMC's Code places on registered nurses to help people exercise their rights, protect their freedoms and work in collaboration with other members of the care team.

Activities: brief outline answers

Activity 4.1

One way to approach the question of the rights of informal patients is from the standpoint of human rights. You will remember that in Chapter 2 we looked at these basic fundamental rights and entitlements, which belong to all of us. These include rights such as the right to life, the right to liberty and the right to family and private life. Being an informal patient on a ward can impact on any of these fundamental rights, for example by being cared for on a locked ward where a patient isn't free to come and go from the ward. You may also have considered more particular patient's rights, such as rights of access to healthcare (that is, not to be discriminated against on various grounds), rights to standards of care, to be treated with dignity and respect, to be involved in decisions about care and treatment and to confidentiality.

Activity 4.3

The nature of the classification of mental disorder is subject to amendment, revision, reclassification and sometimes disagreement. There are, for example, two main diagnostic manuals used in the UK (the 10th Revision of the *International Classification of Diseases* (ICD 10) and the American Psychiatric Association's *Diagnostic and Statistical Manual* (DSM-V)). An approach which leaves 'mental disorder' broadly defined is sufficient because it allows those involved in decision making to draw upon the appropriate evidence base in making their judgements. The Codes of Practice, in slightly different ways, both nonetheless emphasise the importance of good clinical practice in deciding whether a person has a disorder or disability of mind (England 3.2; Wales 2.8).

Activity 4.4

Some of the points that you may have noticed are that there are different groups of forms for each of the sections and these should not be confused with one another. Compared with many other official documents, the forms are relatively brief and require only the bare minimum of information regarding the identity and authority of those completing them as well as about the patient. Some of the forms call for explanations or reasons to be given about actions taken or judgements made and these should be completed where they apply. Each form requires a dated signature which is extremely important.

Further reading

Department of Health (2008) *Code of Practice: Mental Health Act 1983.* London: TSO.

Especially Chapters 4, 5, 12 and 13 (England) or Chapters 5, 8 and 10 (Wales).

Department of Health (2008) *Reference Guide to the Mental Health Act 1983.* London: TSO.

For more detailed reading on the main provisions of the MHA.

Useful websites

http://www.dh.gov.uk/en/Publicationsandstatistics/Publications/PublicationsPolicyAndGuidance/DH_089275

For details of patient information leaflets produced by the Department of Health.

http://www.mentalhealthlaw.co.uk/Mental_Health_Act_1983_Statutory_Forms

For a list of all of the forms currently in use in England.

http://www.wales.nhs.uk/sites3/page.cfm?orgid=816&pid=33957

For information leaflets for patients detained in Wales.

http://www.wales.nhs.uk/sites3/page.cfm?orgid=816&pid=33958

For a list of all the forms currently in use in Wales.

Multiple choice questions

1. A voluntary patient is someone who:

   (a) Must only be admitted to a hospital in either the private or voluntary mental health sector and never the National Health Service
   (b) Lacks the capacity to make a decision about whether they need to be in hospital but does not object to being admitted or staying in hospital
   (c) Participates in clinical trials to improve patient services
   (d) Is an informal patient who can give valid consent to be admitted and is agreeable to receiving care and treatment

2. The Mental Health Act 1983 defines 'mental disorder' as:

    (a)   A disturbance of the mind or brain

    (b)   An impairment of, or a disturbance in the functioning of, the mind or brain

    (c)   A disability of the mind

    (d)   Any disorder or disability of the mind

3. Section 2, admission for assessment

    (a)   May last for up to 28 days. There is no right of appeal

    (b)   May last for up to six months. There is a right of appeal at any time

    (c)   May last for 72 hours and requires only one medical recommendation

    (d)   May last for up to 28 days. The patient can appeal within the first 14 days of the detention

4. Which of the following most accurately describes the nurse's holding power (s5(4))? It:

    (a)   Can be applied by any registered nurse, lasts for up to six hours and is renewable

    (b)   Can be applied if in the judgement of the nurse the patient appears to be mentally disordered even if they are not currently receiving treatment for mental disorder

    (c)   Can only be applied under the direction of the most senior clinical nurse on duty at the time that an application is sought

    (d)   Can be applied by a nurse of the prescribed class, is not renewable and the patient must be already receiving treatment in hospital for a mental disorder

Chapter 5
Medical treatment for mental disorder

NMC Standards for Pre-registration Nursing Education

This chapter will address the following competencies:

Domain 1: Professional values

4. All nurses must work in partnership with service users, carers, groups, communities and organisations. They must manage risk, and promote health and wellbeing while aiming to empower choices that promote self-care and safety.

4.1. Mental health nurses must work with people in a way that values, respects and explores the meaning of their individual lived experiences of mental health problems, to provide person-centred and recovery-focused practice.

6. All nurses must understand the roles and responsibilities of other health and social care professionals, and seek to work with them collaboratively for the benefit of all who need care.

Domain 2: Communication and interpersonal skills

7. All nurses must maintain accurate, clear and complete records, including the use of electronic formats, using appropriate and plain language.

Domain 3: Nursing practice and decision making

2. All nurses must possess a broad knowledge of the structure and functions of the human body, and other relevant knowledge from the life, behavioural and social sciences as applied to health, ill health, disability, ageing and death. They must have an in-depth knowledge of common physical and mental health problems and treatments in their own field of practice, including co-morbidity and physiological and psychological vulnerability.

9. All nurses must be able to recognise when a person is at risk and in need of extra support and protection and take reasonable steps to protect them from abuse.

9.1. Mental health nurses must use recovery-focused approaches to care in situations that are potentially challenging, such as times of acute distress; when compulsory measures are used; and in forensic mental health settings. They must seek to maximise service user involvement and therapeutic engagement, using interventions that balance the need for safety with positive risk-taking.

NMC Essential Skills Clusters

This chapter will address the following ESCs:

Cluster: Care, compassion and communication

8. People can trust the newly registered graduate nurse to gain their consent based on sound understanding and informed choice prior to any intervention and that their rights in decision making and consent will be respected and upheld.

By the second progression point

2. Applies principles of consent in relation to restrictions relating to specific client groups and seeks consent for care.
3. Ensures that the meaning of consent to treatment and care is understood by the people or service users.

Entry to the register

5. Works within legal frameworks when seeking consent.
7. Demonstrates respect for the autonomy and rights of people to withhold consent in relation to treatment within legal frameworks and in relation to people's safety.

Cluster: Medicines management

34. People can trust the newly registered graduate nurse to work within legal and ethical frameworks that underpin safe and effective medicines management.

By the second progression point

1. Demonstrates understanding of legal and ethical frameworks relating to safe administration of medicines in practice.

38. People can trust the newly registered graduate nurse to administer medicines safely and in a timely manner, including controlled drugs.

By the second progression point

1. Uses prescription charts correctly and maintains accurate records.

Entry to the register

6. Understands the legal requirements.

Chapter aims

By the end of this chapter you will be able to:

- summarise the different types of treatment that come under the Mental Health Act;
- be aware of the importance of obtaining consent for any care or treatment you provide;

(continued)

continued ...

- describe the law as it applies when giving treatment to people detained in hospital;
- appreciate the importance of the role of the second opinion appointed doctor in acting as a safeguard;
- understand how the law about 'consent to treatment' works for people on supervised community treatment (SCT).

Introduction

Spend only a few days on a mental health ward and you will inevitably hear nurses and other members of the multidisciplinary team referring to 'Part IV', 'the three month rule' or more commonly, 'T3' or 'section 62'. These are references to aspects of the Mental Health Act (MHA) which deal with treatment for mental disorder. Throughout this chapter, as with others, you will encounter terms that are rather formal. We need to use them, however, because it is the language that is used in the Act and therefore language that you will come across during your training. A common problem with using jargon is that it can give the impression that all those who use it have an equally clear and precise understanding of the subject matter. But the law in relation to treating people who are detained under the Act is not always straightforward. This is particularly so in relation to patients who are on SCT. We shall come to that group of patients at the end of the chapter, but we start by looking at the law in relation to patients who are detained in hospital.

Defining medical treatment

As far as the Act is concerned, medical treatment is not only concerned with treatment prescribed by a doctor. Section 145 states that it *includes nursing, psychological intervention and specialist mental health habilitation, rehabilitation and care.*

For clarity, section 145 also adds:

> *Any reference in this Act to medical treatment, in relation to mental disorder, shall be construed as a reference to medical treatment the purpose of which is to alleviate, or prevent a worsening of, the disorder or one or more of its symptoms or manifestations.*

So, a range of interventions carried out by nurses and other professionals come under the broad definition of 'medical treatment'. For a discussion about mental disorder see Chapter 4.

Consent to treatment

The Nursing and Midwifery (NMC) Code of Conduct (2008) requires all registered nurses to:

- *Gain consent before beginning any treatment or care.*
- *Respect and support people's rights to accept or decline treatment and care.*

- *Uphold people's rights to be fully involved in decisions about their care.*
- *Be aware of the legislation regarding mental capacity, ensuring that people who lack capacity remain at the centre of decision making and are fully safeguarded.*

(NMC, 2008)

In Chapter 2 you were introduced to the subject of patients' rights in relation to consent. The *NHS Constitution for England* summarises these as:

- *The right to accept or refuse treatment and not to be given any physical examination or treatment without valid consent. (Where a patient lacks capacity consent must be obtained from a person legally able to act on their behalf, or the treatment must be in their best interests.)*
- *The right to be given information about proposed treatment in advance, including any significant risks and any alternative treatments which may be available, and the risks involved in doing nothing.*

(Department of Health, 2010a)

These rights apply to all patients and are founded on both common and statute law. To treat patients without their consent may constitute an assault unless it is authorised by the law in some other way. At this point it is worth stopping and reflecting on the high level of powers that the MHA places in the hands of treating teams. As you will read later in the chapter, it enables the treatment not only of patients who consent to be treated but also of patients who lack capacity to consent and even patients who have capacity to consent but refuse to do so. However, in order to ensure these powers are not misused the Act also sets out a number of procedures that need to be followed when consent cannot be given. In order to act lawfully it will be important that you know when and how these apply. These procedures set out situations in which consent is always required as well as the circumstances in which treatment can be given without it. These sections also lay down rules that must be followed so only that treatment which is necessary is given to a patient where consent has not been, or cannot be, obtained.

Case study

In R (PS) *v.* G (Responsible Medical Officer) *a patient, B, who suffered from a psychotic disorder, was convicted of rape and detained under section 37(41) at Broadmoor prison, made a human rights challenge against a decision of his responsible medical officer to treat him with anti-psychotic medication to which he did not consent. The judge did not uphold the challenge, in this case, but stated that the treating team had a duty to consider, amongst other things, if there is a less invasive treatment that is likely to give the same benefits, the degree of resistance to the treatment, the likely efficacy of the treatment, the risk the patient poses to themselves and others, the consequence of not giving the treatment and any adverse effects of the treatment. When the case reached the court of appeal, they agreed that in this case the treatment was lawful but also added that in such cases medical ethics and the common law required the treatment to be in the person's best interest and that this included a consideration of the purpose for which the person is detained and their need for recovery.*

As can be seen from this case, it is not sufficient to generalise treatment powers of the MHA; rather, the specifics of each case need to be considered and decisions made on this basis. Decisions to treat without consent should not be taken lightly. For example, none of the powers that the Act gives you entitle you to set aside your obligations to work co-operatively with patients. You will always have an overriding and ongoing duty to uphold the Code of Conduct at all times and therefore seek to obtain consent even where the law provides that you can administer treatment without it. It is extremely important, therefore, that you are familiar with the precise situations in which the MHA's provisions apply so that you do not inadvertently stray outside the parameters of the law. Any nurse who fails to ensure that there is a proper legal basis for their care will not only have breached the requirements of the NMC Code, but they will have behaved unlawfully and also risk prosecution.

Understanding Part IV and Part IVa of the MHA

Nurses sometimes think that the 'consent to treatment provisions' are only concerned with medicines given to detained patients. Although that is an important aspect, these two parts of the Act, 4 and 4A (the latter added as part of the 2007 amendments) deal with several other areas as well as medication. Different sections within Part IV apply to different groups of patients, some to detained, some to informal patients.

You will need to understand the purpose of each section as well as its scope and limitations. We will first introduce you to each of the sections which relate to detained patients (Part IV) and then discuss the sections that deal with community patients (Part IVa).

Which patients are included in Part IV?

As section 56 makes clear, different groups of patients come under the umbrella of Part IV. Some sections in this part *only* apply to detained patients, others to informal patients as well. There is no simple way to remember which section applies to which group but there are some factors which will help you in understanding why certain provisions apply to some patients and not others. These are: the type of treatment being proposed, the urgency of the treatment, the type of detention order, whether the patient is informal, and the patient's age. Table 5.1 identifies whether the consent to treatment provisions apply to a particular section. If they do not apply then a patient has the same right to refuse treatment as an informal patient.

Activity 5.1   *Team working*

Read the summaries listed here, refer to Table 5.1, and state whether the consent to treatment provisions apply or not in each case.

1. Jo has been detained at a hospital place of safety following the police using their powers under section 136.
2. James was detained under section 4 and his general practitioner (GP) has just attended the hospital and completed the second medical recommendation.

---

3. Ruth has a diagnosis of psychotic disorder, has been arrested for arson and has been remanded to a hospital for a report on her mental health, under section 35.
4. Simon has dementia and has been detained under section 2 following a deterioration and being found in conditions of considerable self-neglect at home.
5. Michael has a psychotic disorder and history of not taking medication and relapsing. He is placed on a CTO after being discharged from hospital to live in supported accommodation.

A brief outline answer to this activity is provided at the end of the chapter.

MHA section	Description	Part IV applies	Comment
2	Admission for assessment	Yes	
3	Admission for treatment	Yes	
4	Emergency admission for assessment	No	When second medical recommendation received section 4 becomes section 2 and Part IV applies
5(2/4)	Application for detention of someone already in hospital	No	
7	Guardianship	No	
17(A)	Patient subject to a community treatment order (CTO)	No	
17(E)	Patient subject to CTO recalled to hospital	Yes	
35	Remand to hospital for a report on an accused person's mental state	No	
36	Remand to hospital of an accused person for treatment	Yes	
37	Hospital order	Yes	If section 37 is used as a guardianship order Part IV does not apply
37/41	Hospital order with restrictions	Yes	
38	Interim hospital order	Yes	
45A	Hospital and limitation directions	Yes	
47	Transfer to hospital of prisoner serving sentence	Yes	
47/49	Transfer order with restrictions	Yes	

(continued)

Table 5.1   (continued)

MHA section	Description	Part IV applies	Comment
48	Removal to hospital of other prisoners	Yes	
135	Removal of patient under warrant to a place of safety	No	
136	Mentally disordered person found in a public place	No	

Table 5.1: Sections which fall within or outside Part IV (apart from s57 that applies to all patients) consent to treatment provisions.

Section 57 (treatment requiring consent and a second opinion)

This section provides an important protection for all patients (both informal and detained) where neurosurgery or other specified forms of invasive/non-reversible treatments are being planned to treat an individual's mental illness.

For treatment to be given, first of all the patient *must consent* to the treatment. Next a second opinion appointed doctor (SOAD) and two other independent people appointed by the regulatory authority must certify that the patient understands *the nature, purpose and likely effects of the treatment being proposed* (s57). The SOAD must also consult two people who are professionally involved in the patient's treatment (statutory consultees). If satisfied that the criteria have been met, they then issue a certificate of 'consent to treatment and second opinion' (England Form T1; Wales Form CO1). Without this, treatment under this section *cannot* be given.

The safeguard is rarely used in practice as neurosurgery is now carried out only in exceptional circumstances with only one or two procedures a year across the UK (HIW, 2011).

Concept summary: SOAD

A SOAD has a specialised role which is often misunderstood by both patients and healthcare professionals. Any patient is entitled to request a second opinion, but the MHA requires, for some patients, that a *statutory second opinion* must be completed before treatment can be given. The statutory second opinion can only be carried out by a doctor who has been specifically appointed for the purpose under the MHA. Neither the patient nor a hospital are allowed to appoint a SOAD; they can only be appointed by the relevant regulatory authority (in practice this means either the Care Quality Commission (CQC) (England) or Welsh ministers). A SOAD's role is to act as a safeguard to ensure that only appropriate treatment is given to those patients who require it (but who may either not wish to consent or be unable to give their consent). They carry out their work by interviewing the patient, speaking to the person in charge of the patient's treatment and consulting two healthcare professionals who are involved in the patient's care and treatment (the statutory consultees). If a SOAD approves treatment they have a legal duty to give reasons for the decision, which the responsible clinician (RC) must then communicate to the patient unless the impact it would have on the patient's mental state justifies not doing so.

A SOAD has the power to challenge the suitability of a proposed treatment plan and they may place conditions on any certificate they issue (such as a time limit, or for electro-convulsive therapy (ECT) the maximum number of treatments authorised).

They also have the power to refuse to issue a certificate. In this case the proposed treatment cannot be given. Such instances are rare in practice and the Code (England 26.64; Wales 18.32) advises the person in charge of the patient's treatment and the SOAD to come to an agreement regarding the proposed treatment wherever possible. In *Monitoring the Mental Health Act 2011/12* the CQC (2013) published details of the outcome of SOAD visits for 2011/12. In 29 per cent of cases the visit led to a change in medication and/or ECT, and in 68 per cent of cases it led to no change. The data was not available for 3 per cent of cases.

Concept summary: statutory consultee

A statutory consultee is someone who a SOAD must talk to before they can complete their opinion. For detained patients, one consultee must be a nurse (s57(3)), so it is likely that as a registered nurse you will act as a consultee. For patients subject to SCT the rules are slightly different and there is no requirement that a nurse is one of the consultees. But, as you are likely to be closely involved in the care of such patients you may well be asked to undertake the role of consultee here too. For both groups of patients the person in charge of the patient's treatment (or the RC if there is one) is barred from acting as a consultee for obvious reasons.

The role of the consultee is the same regardless of the reason for the SOAD consultation. The Code (England 24.52; Wales 18.22) states that:

Statutory consultees may expect to have a private discussion with the SOAD and to be listened to with consideration. Among the issues that the consultees should consider commenting on are:

- *the proposed treatment and the patient's ability to consent to it;*
- *their understanding of the past and present views and wishes of the patient;*

- *other treatment options and the way in which the decision on the treatment proposal was arrived at;*
- *the patient's progress and the views of the patient's carers;*
- *where relevant, the implications of imposing treatment on a patient who does not want it and the reasons why the patient is refusing treatment.*

It is the hospital's responsibility to identify the people who will act as consultees and let the regulatory authority know this at the time of making the request for a second opinion. You should know in advance that you are being asked to undertake this role and you can expect to be involved in deciding whether you are a suitable person to act as a consultee. If you think that another nurse is better placed to talk about the patient's care and treatment than you, make sure that the SOAD is aware of this before they attend. Any hold-ups (by for example not being able to see the statutory consultees) should be avoided because the SOAD is unable to complete their opinion without talking to the two consultees beforehand.

Scenario

Beth is the named nurse for Mary who is being treated with medication for a depressive illness. However, Mary is considered to lack capacity to consent to the treatment and, as it is coming up to three months treatment under detention, has been referred for a SOAD assessment. As named nurse, Beth has been named as a consultee. However, she has only just been appointed named nurse on return from maternity leave. The previous named nurse still works on the ward and knows the patient well. After discussing the case with the previous named nurse it is agreed she is in a better place to be the consultee and is named as such.

A SOAD has a legal duty to record the names of those he or she has consulted on the relevant statutory form. It is both accepted nursing practice and a requirement of the Code (England 24.54; Wales 18.23) that you write your own summary of your discussion with the SOAD in the patient's notes.

Section 58 (treatment requiring consent or a section opinion)

The three month rule

This section is one that you will come across regularly in all types of settings where detained patients are cared for. It states that a patient who is detained under one of the sections where Part IV applies (see above) can be given medicine *without their consent* for up to three months. All detained patients who are not included in Part IV cannot be given medicines without their consent unless it is an emergency. The three month period starts when a patient first receives medicine and not the date on which the person was detained. This is sometimes known as the 'three month rule'.

After three months

After a patient has received medicine for three months they only continue to be given medicine lawfully if one of two conditions has been met.

1. If a patient consents, then the approved clinician (AC) in charge of their treatment (in some cases a SOAD, see below) completes a statutory form (England T2; Wales CO2). This form also records that the AC has certified that the patient has the capacity to make this decision because they have been assessed as *understanding the nature, purpose and likely effects* of the treatment being proposed. A detained patient who has given their consent in this way retains their right to withdraw it at any time in which case treatment cannot be given (unless in an emergency).
2. Alternatively, if a patient cannot consent, or chooses not to do so and the AC considers it necessary for medicines to be given, then a SOAD must be requested (so that a statutory second opinion can be completed). Form T3 (England) or CO3 (Wales) is used by the SOAD and this provides the lawful authorisation for the treatment to be given.

Activity 5.2 — *Decision making*

Consider the case of Mary mentioned in the scenario above and answer the following questions:

What T form will need to be completed before the three months expires?

Who will complete this?

How many consultees will need to be spoken with and what must one be?

Will Mary be spoken with before the T form is competed?

A brief outline answer to this activity is provided at the end of the chapter.

Administering medicine

You have both legal and professional responsibility to ensure that you administer medicines correctly to any patient. Where a patient's treatment is subject to the requirements of the MHA there are additional checks that you need to carry out. As we have seen, Form T2/CO1 or T3/CO2 gives you the legal authority to continue to give medicines. It is not an order or direction to administer the medicine, however (Code of Practice England 24.68; Wales 17.60). This distinction is important because it means that *every time* you administer medicine to someone under the authority of a 'T2' or 'T3' you need to be personally satisfied that it is appropriate to give it. So that you do not inadvertently give medicines to a patient without lawful authority, the Code of Practice (England 24.71; Wales 17.30) advises that a copy of the relevant form is placed alongside the patient's medicine chart. You should check the form each time medicines are given to make sure that the authorisation is still valid. If it is not, then you must seek advice immediately.

Giving medicines covertly

This means administering medicines by deception, in a secretive or disguised manner (usually by adding to food or drink). The NMC's Code requires that you always act in ways in which the trust that patients place in our profession can be justified and demonstrated. Amongst other things, the Code says nurses must therefore *be open and honest, act with integrity and uphold the reputation of your profession* (NMC, 2008). This is challenged when medicines are given to patients covertly. In its position statement (see **http://www.nmc.uk.org/Nurses-and-midwives/ Regulation-in-practice/Medicines-management-and-prescribing/Covert-administration-of- medicines**) the NMC rightly recognises that this is a complex issue. Unlike the administration of medicines against a person's consent, giving medicines covertly involves deception. Although choosing to give medicines covertly should, always, only ever be done with the patient's best interests in mind, the practice nonetheless cannot escape creating concerns among patients, relatives and nurses alike.

We have, up to now, assumed that when you are involved in giving medicines to patients you will be doing so in an open and transparent way. Even if, for example, you need to restrain someone in order to administer medicine, it is obvious what you are doing. Put another way, we have assumed you will not be involved in any act, such as covert administration of medicine, which seeks to deceive a patient. Giving medicines covertly breaks the bond of trust between patient and nurse because the nurse has chosen to act in a way which conceals her intentions. There may be rare occasions when it can be justified, but these occasions are never routine.

Concept summary: the NMC and covert administration of medicine

The NMC's position statement includes the following points which you need to be aware of:

- The best interests of the patient or client are always paramount.
- Any act of covert administration should not conflict with a nurse's duty to act at all times in such a manner as to justify public trust and confidence.
- A nurse is personally accountable for a decision to administer medicines covertly.
- The interests of the registrant, team or organisation should not determine any decision to administer medicines. There should be a framework within every clinical setting for open multi-professional discussion and access to legal advice if necessary. These discussions and any possible resulting action must be documented in the current care plan.
- Covert administration should not occur without the knowledge and support of other members of the care team.
- In developing policies and procedures on covert administration, health professionals should ensure they have obtained legal advice.

- Covert administration should be recorded fully in the patient's notes.
- Nurses involved in the practice of administering medicines covertly should be fully aware of the aims, intent and implications of such treatment.
- A decision to give medicines covertly should always be as a last resort, contingency action taken once an individual assessment of the patient has been carried out.

The ethical and moral concerns should never be minimised but, clearly, giving medicines covertly in some circumstances is lawful. You should, however, never give medicines covertly to any detained patient who is capable of consenting to their treatment. Such deception is unlawful. It may also be permissible to administer medicines covertly under the Mental Capacity Act if it is judged as being in the best interests of the patient.

Case study: Nurse secretly sedated vulnerable residents

A care home nurse who secretly gave elderly residents powerful sedatives was struck off following an NMC hearing. The nurse kept a secret supply of sedatives and she was observed adding these to the residents' usual medicines by a healthcare assistant who reported his concerns to the home's manager. The nurse admitted carrying Temazepam not prescribed for residents. She was found guilty of dishonestly obtaining Temazepam, administering unprescribed medication, sleeping on shift, removing call bells and applying extra incontinence pads. The NMC disciplinary panel found that the vast majority of the nurse's actions were for her own benefit at the expense of the residents.
(This is Dorset, *30 September 2009*)

Section 58A (electro-convulsive therapy (ECT) etc.)

The amendments to the MHA resulted in some important changes to the rules regarding the administration of ECT and a new section (58A) was inserted into the Act. One important overall effect is that ECT now cannot be given to an individual who has the capacity to consent to it but who has not consented (Department of Health, 2008a, 16.44). In addition the three month rule now no longer applies to ECT and there must be a treatment certificate in all cases.

This new section also brings in different levels of protection for patients aged under 18 compared to those over 18.

For a detained patient over 18 who is capable of giving their consent, ECT can only be given if either the AC or a SOAD has certified that the patient is capable of understanding the nature, purpose and likely effects of the treatment and has consented to it (s58A (3)). This is done on a T4 form. If a patient is incapable of consenting to the treatment it can only be given if a SOAD (and never the AC) has certified that it is appropriate that the treatment is given. This is done on a T6 form. Even then, ECT can only be given if doing so does not conflict with an advance decision. If a patient is over 18 and not detained then none of these rules apply and the rules for ECT are the same as for other medical treatments.

For someone under 18 (whether they are an informal or detained patient) ECT can only be given on the written authorisation of a SOAD (whether or not the person consents). Where such a patient has given their consent then the SOAD's job is to certify that the person has capacity to consent, has consented and provides a statement that the treatment is appropriate. This is done on form T5. If the young person cannot consent then the SOAD certifies that they are incapable of giving their consent, but that the treatment is appropriate. This is done on form T6. The SOAD must also declare that giving ECT would not go against a decision made on behalf of the young person by the Court of Protection.

Activity 5.3   *Critical thinking*

Consider the following scenarios and name the appropriate treatment certificate that would need to be in place for ECT to be given.

John is very depressed. He is 42 and his RC is considering ECT as other treatments are not proving effective and ECT has worked in the past. However, John lacks capacity to consent. He is currently detained under section 2.

Rachael is 17 and has a very severe depressive disorder. She is detained under section 3 and has stopped eating and drinking. Her RC believes she has capacity to consent to ECT and is considering it as a possible treatment.

Simon is 58 and has a long history of depressive episodes. ECT has been very effective for him in the past and he is very supportive of its use. He is an informal patient.

A brief outline answer to this activity is provided at the end of the chapter.

Section 62 (urgent treatment)

In urgent situations treatment for mental disorder can be given to a detained patient without following the procedures in sections 57, 58 and 58A above. An AC can only authorise treatment under this section for those people who are detained under one of the sections to which Part IV applies (see above). If urgent treatment needs to be given to any other patient then the legal basis for such treatment would come either from the common law or the Mental Capacity Act.

For section 62 to apply to medication or section 57 treatments then it must be given in order to either:

- *save the patient's life;*
- *prevent a serious deterioration of the patient's condition, and the treatment does not have unfavourable physical or psychological consequences which cannot be reversed;*
- *alleviate serious suffering by the patient, and the treatment does not have unfavourable physical or psychological consequences which cannot be reversed and does not entail significant physical hazard;*
- *prevent patients behaving violently or being a danger to themselves or others, and the treatment represents the minimum interference necessary for that purpose, does not have unfavourable physical or psychological consequences which cannot be reversed and does not entail significant physical hazard.*

(Code of Practice England 24.3; Wales 17.55)

For ECT, urgent treatment can be given without following the section 58A procedures but it must be given for one of the first two purposes listed above.

Unlike section 57 or section 58 above, there are no statutory forms which are completed when an AC authorises treatment under section 62. The Code (England 24.32–24.37; Wales 17.54–17.58) is rightly concerned to ensure that instances of the use of section 62 are properly documented, in order that its use can be audited and available to external scrutiny. The Code places responsibility on the hospital's managers and the clinician in charge of the treatment to ensure this happens. You will frequently be responsible for administering treatment under this power, so you have an important duty in ensuring that the use of this power is properly recorded each time it is used. It will also be important that you are aware of the procedures in your hospital for identifying which ACs are available to authorise such treatments in urgent situations.

Withdrawal of consent or change in capacity

The MHA enables the patient to withdraw consent that they had previously given, at any time. In addition, a patient's consent may no longer be valid due to them losing capacity. In these cases a T2 treatment certificate will no longer be valid. However, treatment may continue, whilst a certificate is sought, providing an AC considers stopping it would cause serious suffering to the patient.

Section 63 (treatment not requiring consent)

This section allows any medical treatment which is not covered by sections 57, 58 or 58A to be given without consent to any patient detained to whom Part IV applies. As we learned earlier, the definition of medical treatment is wide and so a range of interventions can be given without consent, including those therapeutic interventions given by nurses as well as other health professionals. Your overriding professional responsibility to work co-operatively with patients is *never* bypassed by this provision. You ought always to try to seek consent for any care that you give to a patient detained under the Act as a matter of principle even if the law permits you to provide care without it. Examples of such treatments include self-care needed due to the effects of depression or dementia, interventions to prevent self-harm or address its consequences (including overdoses), treating physical conditions that are causing or worsening the core mental disorder (e.g. infections) and nasogastric feeding to address the consequences of an eating disorder.

Human rights and treatment without consent

Administering treatment without consent engages a patient's right to private and family life and if serious enough could also engage a person's right not to be subject to inhumane and degrading treatment. In *X* v. *Finland*, the European Court of Human Rights, in 2012, considered the case of a Finnish patient who was treated without consent. Under the relevant Finnish law, following a patient's detention there were no further procedures or safeguards governing their medical treatment. The court held that this did not give X sufficient protection against misuse of power and therefore violated their human rights. The case highlights the degree of control that treating teams have over detained patients and the importance of having safeguards surrounding their treatment decisions. The sufficiency of the treatment procedures under the MHA has not yet been considered, in this regard, by the European Courts. However, these are the provisions that currently offer protection against the misuse of power to patients detained under the Act. As a nurse you have a duty to uphold the human rights of patients. Ensuring that the treatment provisions are correctly followed and being satisfied that it is appropriate to administer treatment before doing so are key ways that you can do this.

Section summary

So far we have looked at the procedures and safeguards that apply when giving treatment to detained patients in hospital. You have been introduced to the role of the SOAD as well as the statutory consultee. We have discussed the importance of the nurse's role in relation to administering treatment, specifically medicines. The different rules that need to be followed depending on the type of treatment being given and the circumstances in which the treatment is being given have been summarised. We now turn to look at that part of the Act which deals with consent to treatment for patients subject to SCT.

Understanding Part IVa

Which patients are included in Part IVa?

Part IVa deals with what the Act refers to as community patients. This means *only* those patients who have been made subject to SCT because they are on a CTO. Therefore, patients subject to guardianship or those who may be living in the community on leave from hospital (s17 leave) or informal patients are not included here.

There are approximately 4000 patients who are on SCT at any one time. There is widespread misunderstanding about the legal powers around patients subject to CTOs, even among the professionals who care for such patients. This may be because the law is still relatively new, but equally the law itself is not easy to understand: there are 11 different sections (64A–64K) which deal solely with this area. We discuss SCT in more detail in Chapter 7, but here we shall discuss only the issues around consent to treatment for this group.

As with detained patients, there will be those patients on SCT who have the capacity to consent to treatment and those who do not. There are different rules which apply to each sub-group. There are also different rules depending on whether or not a patient on SCT has been recalled to hospital or has had their CTO revoked. We shall look at each of these situations so that you understand what rights patients have and what you may, or may not, be permitted to do in giving treatment.

Patients on SCT who consent to receive their treatment

Someone who is on SCT and has the capacity to consent to receive treatment must not be given that treatment if they withdraw their consent. The MHA does not permit you to give medicines to patients on SCT without their consent as it does in some cases for a patient who is detained in hospital. In effect, a patient on SCT who consents to receive their treatment is in exactly the same position as an informal patient. Only if a patient on SCT has been recalled to hospital can they be given treatment against their wishes.

Case study

Simon Lockwood had been on SCT for about one week when his community nurse, Ray Carberry, called to see him. He had previously been detained in hospital under section 3 and had refused to agree to the treatment proposed by his AC. A SOAD carried out a second opinion visit and after interviewing Simon concluded that he had the capacity to consent to treatment, was refusing to do so, but that the treatment proposed by his doctor was appropriate. The SOAD certified that it was appropriate for the treatment to be given. Although the nursing team sought to gain Simon's co-operation it was necessary to restrain him to give him an injection. Following a period of leave he was then transferred onto a CTO. The nurse called to see him to administer another injection authorised as part of his treatment plan. Simon, however, refused to have it arguing that it made him feel too drowsy. Although he said he did feel less 'spaced out' as a result of the medicine he'd been given and that the medicine had helped him think a bit more clearly, he was determined that he didn't want to receive another injection so soon after the last one. Ray tried to persuade Simon to accept his treatment. Simon felt very strongly about the matter and Ray left without giving the injection. Later that day he discussed the visit with the AC in charge of Simon's care.

Patients on SCT who cannot consent to receive their treatment

A patient who needs medicine but cannot (rather than does not) consent to receive it can be given their medicines with the consent of a Court of Protection appointed deputy, an attorney (under Lasting Power of Attorney) with authority to make the decision or in line with a Court of Protection direction. It can also be given without anyone's consent providing it does not conflict with an advance decision to refuse treatment, a decision of the Court of Protection, a court appointed deputy or an attorney (Lasting Power of Attorney), no force is needed or force is needed but the patient does not object. In practice it can be difficult to sensibly understand the distinction between force used where there is no objection or force used when there is an objection. One example could be the need to hold a person still, due to a physical disorder, but the person does not display any behaviour that indicates objection. However, perhaps a safer rule of thumb would be not to proceed if there is any behaviour that indicates an objection and the person doesn't respond to legitimate persuasion.

Case study

James has a psychotic disorder, is under a CTO, lacks capacity to consent to his depot medication and is due an injection. You attend his house, as arranged. He states that he is tired of having the medication and its side effects. You talk through with him the likelihood of a relapse if he does not comply with his treatment. However, he is still resistant, so you agree to give him a chance to think about it and come back the following day. When you return the following day, he has had a chance to think about it further, agrees to the injection and co-operates throughout.

Patients on SCT who need emergency treatment

This section (s64G) is similar to that for detained patients (s62 above). There are a number of conditions which apply and these are:

- *When giving the treatment, the person reasonably believes that the patient lacks capacity to consent to it or, as the case may be, is not competent to consent to it.*
- *The treatment is immediately necessary.*
- *If it is necessary to use force against the patient in order to give the treatment:*
  - *the treatment needs to be given in order to prevent harm to the patient; and*
  - *the use of such force is a proportionate response to the likelihood of the patient's suffering harm, and to the seriousness of that harm.*

(s64G)

In practice, any use of force will have to be extremely carefully considered given that an emergency will, by definition, have occurred in a setting other than a hospital. All of the risks to the patient will need to be carefully assessed because the patient's safety is paramount. If a patient has the capacity to refuse treatment then this section does not allow you to use any force to give treatment whatever the emergency. In such situations, if it is necessary to give treatment urgently, then either the patient can be recalled to hospital or treatment could be given under another authority (such as the common law or Mental Capacity Act).

Statutory second opinions for people on SCT

As with detained patients, certificate requirements also apply to patients on CTOs. Someone who is on SCT for longer than 28 days must have such a certificate. This period can be longer if the CTO started within the first three months of medicines being given, in which case authorisation is not needed until the three month period ends. For patients who have capacity to consent and do so the RC must complete a CTO12. For patients who lack capacity to consent then a SOAD must complete a CTO11. The SOAD's job here is similar to that which they carry out for patients detained under Part IV; they will interview the patient, talk over the treatment plan with the AC and talk to two statutory consultees. As already indicated, a patient who has capacity and refuses to consent cannot be treated whilst they remain a community patient on a CTO. Where a certificate has been issued you should ensure that the form is valid every time you give someone medicine. It is also necessary for you to follow any conditions that the SOAD may have written as part of the certificate.

Patients on SCT who are recalled to hospital

If a patient on SCT has been recalled to hospital, different rules apply and medicines can, in certain situations, be given without their consent. If it is within the first month of them being placed on a CTO or within three months since first being given medication under their initial detention (that led to the CTO) then a certificate is not needed. If a CTO11 is in place, a SOAD may have decided to include medicines to be given to the patient once they have been recalled to hospital (together with any conditions on that treatment). If a CTO11 is not in place or if a SOAD has not authorised any such treatment, then it may be authorised under the other provisions of Part IV, as detailed above. This includes section 62. In addition, treatment can be continued pending compliance with a treatment certificate providing an AC considers stopping it would cause serious suffering to the patient. Finally, the provisions of section 64(G), described above, also apply to recalled patients.

Section summary

Part IVa is solely concerned with the rules and safeguards around treatment for patients subject to SCT. We have seen that the rules are somewhat complex. Generally someone on SCT, whether or not they are able to consent to treatment, cannot be given any treatment in situations in which they are refusing to receive it. There are certain circumstances where treatment can be given in an emergency (as with detained patients). You are not permitted to give treatment to a patient subject to SCT who is refusing to receive it, but if someone has been recalled to hospital then treatment can be given against a patient's wishes, if certain conditions are met.

Chapter summary

We have looked in depth at the various rules that apply to giving detained patients different kinds of treatment under the MHA. We have revisited the issue of patients' rights in relation to consent to treatment. You have been introduced to the procedures that must be followed to check that patients are only given treatment that is necessary for them to receive, particularly when they do not, or cannot, consent to receive their treatment. We have described the specialised role of the SOAD and you have learned how important the role of the statutory consultee is in helping a SOAD carry out their role.

Activities: brief outline answers

Activity 5.1

Person	Does Part IV apply (not including s57 treatments which apply to all patients)
Jo	No
James	Yes
Ruth	No
Simon	Yes
Michael	No

Activity 5.2

A T3 certificate will need to be completed. A second opinion appointed doctor (SOAD) will complete the form. Two consultees will need to be involved and one will need to be a nurse. Mary will be spoken with by the SOAD.

Activity 5.3

Person	Treatment certificate
John	T6
Rachael	T5
Simon	None as an informal patient

Further reading

Care Quality Commission (CQC) (2013) *Monitoring the Mental Health Act 2011/12*. Newcastle: Care Quality Commission. **http://www.cqc.org.uk/sites/default/files/media/documents/cqc_mentalhealth_2011_12_main_final_web.pdf**

Information on the outcome of SOAD visits and findings in relation to them.

Department of Health (2008) *Reference Guide to the Mental Health Act 1983*. London: TSO.

Department of Health (2008) *Code of Practice: Mental Health Act 1983*. London: TSO.

Information on the treatment provisions of the MHA.

Useful websites

http://www.cqc.org.uk/organisations-we-regulate/mental-health-services/mental-health-act-guidance/second-opinion-appointed

Information about the SOAD service.

Multiple choice questions

1. Who can appoint a second opinion appointed doctor?

    (a)   Service user/patient
    (b)   The Care Quality Commission
    (c)   The hospital
    (d)   A patient's family

2. Part IV (consent to treatment) of the MHA applies in which cases?

    (a)   A patient on community treatment order
    (b)   Someone found mentally disordered in the street
    (c)   A patient on community treatment order recalled to hospital
    (d)   Someone admitted as an emergency

3. The 'three month rule' on administering medicines is taken to be three months from when?

    (a)   From when the medicine was first administered under that period of detention
    (b)   From when the patient was first admitted
    (c)   From when the patient refused consent
    (d)   From when the medicine was last administered

4. Under what circumstances can a patient under supervised community treatment *not* be given treatment against their wishes?

    (a)   If they are recalled to hospital
    (b)   If they have capacity and do not consent
    (c)   If the community treatment order is revoked
    (d)   In an emergency

Chapter 6
Leave from hospital

NMC Standards for Pre-registration Nursing Education

This chapter will address the following competencies:

Domain 1: Professional values

2.   All nurses must practise in a holistic, non-judgmental, caring and sensitive manner that avoids assumptions; supports social inclusion; recognises and respects individual choice; and acknowledges diversity. Where necessary, they must challenge inequality, discrimination and exclusion from access to care.

2.1. Mental health nurses must practise in a way that addresses the potential power imbalances between professionals and people experiencing mental health problems, including situations when compulsory measures are used, by helping people exercise their rights, upholding safeguards and ensuring minimal restrictions on their lives. They must have an in depth understanding of mental health legislation and how it relates to care and treatment of people with mental health problems.

Domain 3: Nursing practice and decision-making

7.   All nurses must be able to recognise and interpret signs of normal and deteriorating mental and physical health and respond promptly to maintain or improve the health and comfort of the service user, acting to keep them and others safe.

7.1. Mental health nurses must provide support and therapeutic interventions for people experiencing critical and acute mental health problems. They must recognise the health and social factors that can contribute to crisis and relapse and use skills in early intervention, crisis resolution and relapse management in a way that ensures safety and security and promotes recovery.

8.   All nurses must provide educational support, facilitation skills and therapeutic nursing interventions to optimise health and wellbeing. They must promote self-care and management whenever possible, helping people to make choices about their healthcare needs, involving families and carers where appropriate, to maximise their ability to care for themselves.

8.1. Mental health nurses must practise in a way that promotes the self-determination and expertise of people with mental health problems, using a range of approaches and tools that aid wellness and recovery and enable self-care and self-management.

NMC Essential Skills Clusters

This chapter will address the following ESCs:

Cluster: Care, compassion and communication

1. As partners in the care process, people can trust a newly registered graduate nurse to provide collaborative care based on the highest standards, knowledge and competence.

Entry to the register

11. Acts as a role model in developing trusting relationships, within professional boundaries.

2. People can trust the newly registered graduate nurse to engage in person centred care empowering people to make choices about how their needs are met when they are unable to meet them for themselves.

Entry to the register

10. Recognises situations and acts appropriately when a person's choice may compromise their safety or the safety of others.

11. Uses strategies to manage situations where a person's wishes conflict with nursing interventions necessary for the person's safety.

Cluster: Organisational aspects of care

6. People can trust the newly registered graduate nurse to engage therapeutically and actively listen to their needs and concerns, responding using skills that are helpful, providing information that is clear, accurate, meaningful and free from jargon.

First progression point

2. Records information accurately and clearly on the basis of observation and communication.

Entry to the register

13. Uses appropriate and relevant communication skills to deal with difficult and challenging circumstances, for example, responding to emergencies, unexpected occurrences, saying 'no', dealing with complaints, resolving disputes, de-escalating aggression, conveying 'unwelcome news'.

18. People can trust a newly registered graduate nurse to enhance the safety of service users and identify and actively manage risk and uncertainty in relation to people, the environment, self and others.

Entry to the register

13. Works within legal and ethical frameworks to promote safety and positive risk taking.

Chapter aims

By the end of this chapter you will be able to:

- discuss the nature and purpose of section 17 leave in a patient's recovery and its associated risks;
- say who can authorise section 17 leave, what they must consider and the conditions that can be attached;
- reflect on the balance between autonomy and safety in relation to section 17 leave;
- discuss the role and powers of an escort, and the nurse's role in ensuring safe practice in respect of section 17 leave;
- understand leave in relation to informal patients.

Introduction

Being in need of psychiatric treatment does not mean a person should be treated as a prisoner; at the same time being in an acute stage of a psychiatric illness can be a time of increased risk. As a nurse you will be a part of a team that seeks a difficult balance between autonomy and safety. In this regard, decisions about leave from the ward will strike at the very heart of a patient's rights to care and liberty and the dilemmas inherent in being a nurse. Your role will need to be strongly grounded in the core values of nursing and sound clinical decision making.

This chapter looks in detail at the provisions of the Mental Health Act (MHA) that allow detained patients to leave the hospital in which they are detained. It will help you understand the procedures that must be followed and the consequences of not following them. Throughout, the chapter will explore the processes that underpin decision making and enable you to keep the impact on the patient and other people involved central to your decision making. The chapter also briefly explores the issue of informal patient leave from psychiatric hospitals.

Activity 6.1   *Reflection*

When people are admitted to a psychiatric hospital it can have a dramatic effect on their life, even more so when they are detained there. Spend some time reflecting on this and what role time off the ward could have in a person's experience of being in hospital and their recovery, and make a list of your ideas. Now spend some time thinking about, and list, who may be involved in the leave. Finally, spend some time considering, and list, what some of the risks may be. Keep your list and review it as you read the discussions which follow.

There is an outline answer at the end of the chapter.

> ### Case study
>
> *James is a 25-year-old single man who had been living with his parents at the time he was detained in a psychiatric intensive care unit (PICU), after experiencing an episode of acute psychosis. During his time of being unwell in the community he ran into difficulties with his job, family relationships and daily bills, and lost many of the routines that gave structure to his life. As he began to recover in hospital he became more aware of all the things he wanted to put back in place again. He also began to become frustrated with the restrictions that were placed on him in hospital and of having someone else control his life. He knew he needed to take his recovery one step at a time but at times wanted to just run away from the confined space of the ward and experience his freedom again: meet friends, have a drink and do the things he enjoyed. At other times he just wanted to begin again. He was often worried about sharing these thoughts and feelings with the staff as he feared it may mean they saw him as a risk of absconding or not complying with his care plan. His parents wanted to be able to play a more active part in his recovery and enable him to start having overnight leave but they were concerned about how they would cope and what would happen if things went wrong. They were also concerned that James may not always tell them when he experiences difficulties or symptoms of his relapse.*

As can be seen from the case study, having time off the ward will be essential to James rebuilding his life and working towards returning home. Yet there are dangers in the process that will require the professionals involved to engage with James and his family, reach sound assessments and be clear on the purpose of the powers that the MHA 1983 gives them.

The role of leave in a patient's recovery

In the Code of Practice, the purpose principle makes it clear that decisions under the MHA should be made to promote the person's recovery and manage risk. In the Welsh Code the empowerment principle makes it clear that wellbeing and safety should be at the heart of decision making. In Chapter 2 you considered how these values can be implemented to ensure patients' rights are upheld, and saw some of the tensions that can arise when some wishes and needs of patients conflict with legal duties to keep them and others safe.

It is perhaps in the context of considering a patient's leave that you will experience an inherent conflict between risk, autonomy, participation and recovery. You will need to be mindful that the ethical basis of the powers under the MHA is aimed at restoring autonomy through recovery.

The tensions between autonomy, recovery and safety are at the heart of decision making around a patient's leave from the ward. We will now explore the framework the MHA establishes to support this decision making.

Authorised absence

The patient's responsible clinician (RC) has a key role, as detained patients can only leave the hospital if their RC has granted them leave under section 17. For restricted patients, the RC needs the agreement of the Secretary of State before granting such leave. Patients who have been remanded to hospital under sections 35 or 36 of the Act or who are subject to interim hospital orders under section 38 can only be given leave by the court.

The RC can grant leave for specific occasions or for specific or indefinite periods of time. When doing so, they may also set any conditions they consider necessary in the interest of the patient or the protection of other people. As far as is possible, the conditions and the likely consequences of breaking them should be clearly explained to the patient. This protects the patient's rights by ensuring they can foresee the consequences of any choices they make and is an essential part of their participation in their care planning. It can also, on a practical level, reduce the risk of conflict between nursing staff and the patient when the patient wants to take the leave and reduces risk to the patient and others by the misinterpretation of conditions.

Scenario

At a care planning meeting, James asked his RC if he could have leave to visit his friends who live locally. Although his friends lived 12 miles away and the journey involved two bus rides to see them, James considered them as local because they were his closest friends and he was used to spending time with them on regular occasions. His RC was about to authorise leave in the local area. By raising the issue and clarifying the different meanings people give to the same words you were able to start a discussion about the risks involved in James being given this leave. The RC agreed for you and James to spend some time identifying where he would have to go, the risks involved and planning how James could safely take this leave and then discuss the matter further with him. In your planning you consider using a map or glossary of terms, to reduce ambiguity.

In this scenario, although the RC was the one who granted leave for James, your role was essential in ensuring the leave was well planned, risk assessed and promoted James's autonomy. This would have needed skills in assessment, engagement and communication.

Factors to consider when granting leave

As we have discussed, granting leave is about getting the right balance between the benefits and risks involved. Case law requires the RC to record these before granting leave (*G* v. *Central and North West London Mental Health NHS Trust* [2007]).

Activity 6.2   *Decision making*

Make a list of all the factors you think the RC should consider before granting leave. You may want to start with ideas from James's situation. Now look up the Code of Practice paragraph 21.8 (Welsh Code of Practice 28.7) and compare your list to this one.

There is an outline answer at the end of the chapter.

The list in the Code is not exhaustive and the RC will need to identify any other relevant considerations from their knowledge of the patient and information gathered from others. When practising as a nurse you will need to think about your role in providing the RC with the information they need to make these decisions. This will include conversations with and observations of patients, their carers and other third parties. Essential Skills Cluster: Care, compassion and communication standard 6 requires nurses *to provide meaningful and comprehensive reports*. In this context it is important that you ensure key points are not lost amongst incidental facts or by not recording them at all. It is also worth considering the processes of the ward that ensure any significant information not directly given to the RC is summarised and brought to the attention of the RC, when they make decisions.

Escorted leave

When setting conditions, section 17(3) enables the RC to specify that a patient on section 17 leave may be kept in the custody of specific people; this is often referred to as escorted leave. The Act states that this can be an officer of the staff of the hospital in which the patient is detained, of one to which the patient is required to remain as a condition of section 17 leave, or any other person authorised in writing by the detaining organisation. The term 'officer' is not defined in the Act. However, organisations should have policies defining who this can be and should ensure that they are suitably trained, supported and supervised. It will certainly include staff nurses.

The RC recording leave that is granted

The Code of Practice states that hospitals should develop a standard form to record leave that is granted. This will normally include the dates and parameters of the leave and any conditions attached. It may also include to whom the form is given, risks of which nurses need to be aware, a contingency plan and a place for the patient to sign. However, different hospitals may use different systems to manage these aspects of leave. The correct use of this form and the systems that support it are key to ensuring that all parties know what leave a person has, know the conditions attached and what to do if leave goes wrong.

Nurse's discretion in allowing leave

In addition to playing a role in the planning and granting of leave, nurses also have a key role in the safe management of leave at the time the patient takes it. Generally, RCs will authorise short term periods of leave and nurses will often be the ones deciding exactly when that leave is taken. The Code of Practice paragraph 21.17 states that *parameters within which this discretion may be exercised must be clearly set out by the RC* (Welsh Code of Practice 28.13). It gives the examples of these parameters as times of day, places, any restrictions and circumstances in which leave should not go ahead. This can enable flexibility in how leave is taken and ensure the most productive use of the leave for the patient and the most effective and equitable use of nursing staff's time.

> ### Case study
>
> *Hollows is a PICU ward. It has a weekly meeting run by the independent mental health advocate (IMHA) service, at which patients can raise any concerns about the ward culture or environment. For a number of weeks different patients raised the concern that there are never staff members available to take them on escorted leave when they request it. The issue was brought back to the ward managers and staff. As a response a diary sheet of staff availability was produced and times for escorted leave could be booked. This enabled the ward to easily monitor how much leave each patient was taking, ensure there was equity amongst patients and review how staffing levels affected patients' leave.*

Activity 6.3   *Decision making*

Read James's story again and think about how an RC may plan leave at an early stage. It may be that, as a ward nurse, you support a patient to think through these issues before they request leave or that you make a recommendation to the RC. Make notes on:

- what type of leave would be essential as a part of his recovery;
- examples of the place, purpose and times of this leave;
- what risks may be associated with it;
- what conditions and contingency plans could be put in place to manage the risks.

There is an outline answer at the end of the chapter.

Nursing staff not allowing leave

The RC may also set a wider condition that nursing staff can decide not to implement any authorised leave on medical grounds at their discretion. In doing so they may give guidance about what is significant in each specific case, for example, instances of self-harm, refusal of medication or signs of relapse. In the case of James it may be around concerns that his psychosis is returning and that he is masking it. In their guidance on the Mental Health Act, which is currently under review, the Care Quality Commission (CQC) advised that if a nurse has significant concerns before any leave then they should withhold it pending advice from the RC.

In this situation the nurse has a duty both to promote James's recovery, and to ensure his safety and that of others. The nurse also has considerable power over James. As was discussed in Chapter 2, it is essential in upholding James's rights to ensure that any restrictions on him or balanced risk taking is underpinned by sound decision making and not based on personality or emotion. You will need to think about the process you use to make and record these decisions in a way that is clear, concise and transparent. You will also need to be aware of the ward processes that ensure you have contemporaneous and accurate risk assessments to inform your decisions.

Other recording requirements when leave is taken

The Code of Practice advises that a description of the patient should be recorded in case they fail to return. The CQC guidance advises that the following should be recorded: every occasion when leave is taken; the circumstances under which leave is taken (for example, whether the patient is escorted, and if so, by whom); the date and time at which the patient departs; and the date and time by which the patient must return.

Furthermore, in their ninth biannual report their predecessor, the MHA Commission, recommended that nurses only allow authorised leave: following consultation with involved professionals to ensure that the patient's needs are fully assessed and addressed by the care plan, all of which should be recorded in the patient's clinical record; following a detailed risk assessment which is similarly recorded; with carefully considered contingency plans, including contact telephone numbers; with clearly set down parameters, including the time of return; and with clearly set down supervision arrangements (Mental Health Act Commission, 2001, recommendation 36).

Although these are not legal requirements of the MHA, following them will be more likely to lead to safe and transparent decision making.

Keeping those involved in leave informed

As James's story has shown, periods of leave will often involve informal carers and family members. These people will have their own needs, strengths, vulnerabilities, views and concerns. At times they may be depended on to ensure a safe and effective outcome of leave or to communicate their concerns. Within the confines of patient confidentiality those involved in leave should be kept informed and involved in decision making. If the patient does not consent to this, paragraph 21.20 of the Code suggests that the RC s*hould reconsider whether or not it is safe and appropriate to grant leave* (the Welsh Code of Practice is not as explicit but gives guidance on these issues at 28.14 to 28.15).

Reviewing leave

Reviewing leave and allowing a patient to reflect on how their leave went can form a key part of a patient's recovery and ensure their safety. In the case of James this could be how he managed symptoms of psychosis in new situations, how he has established daily routines again, or the impact of his relationships with family. Such a review would have the benefit of helping with forward planning and making contingency plans for a time of crisis or the setting of advance directives about what James wants to happen if he relapses.

Ultimately, the aim is for the person to manage their own leave. You can help by creating opportunities for the patient to reflect on how it is developing, what they want to achieve, and aiming for them to have the right level of participation. This can create, for the patient, some sense of control and anticipation of greater autonomy in the future.

Leave within the hospital

Restricted patients who the Ministry of Justice has decided to detain in a particular unit require section 17 leave to visit other areas of the hospital. Non-restricted patients do not need section 17 leave to cover periods in the hospital grounds or other parts of the same hospital. The only exception to this is when two or more organisations manage different units in the same hospital. In these cases, patients should be granted leave if they are to attend those parts managed by a different organisation.

Section summary

In this section we have explored the planning, granting, management and review of leave, and considered the factors that need to be taken into account to ensure that leave is safely planned, promotes autonomy and recovery and involves the patient in planning. We have looked at how we can support these processes, and the wider link to care planning.

Use of long term leave

Case study

James is now at a stage when he no longer needs to be an inpatient and his return home is being considered. Although he is currently settled and managing his day to day life, his RC remains concerned that he does not always recognise the importance of engaging with his care team and remaining compliant with his medication. James has said that sometimes he only takes his medication because he is under section and he finds the side effects difficult to come to terms with. His RC is of the view that James's history suggests that if he stops his medication he will relapse quickly and the risks are likely to lead to him needing to come back to hospital. The RC is also concerned about the added pressure involved in the process of discharge.

Activity 6.4   *Critical thinking*

Read the case study, and make a list of the positives and negatives of James returning home or remaining on the ward. You will want to revisit these questions when you have finished reading this chapter.

There is an outline answer at the end of the chapter.

We have seen that the RC can set a condition to leave that a patient resides at a specific place. In the 2000s the use of section 17 leave powers was considerably extended by the courts. For example it was held that, in order to meet the criteria for renewal, treatment at a hospital must form a significant component of the treatment plan but this does not have to be as an inpatient (*R. (on the application of DR)* v. *Mersey Care NHS Trust*). This judgement was applied in *R. (on the application of CS)* v. *Mental Health Review Tribunal*. In this case the patient was ruled to meet the requirement of receiving hospital treatment in a situation in which they were required to attend the hospital for weekly sessions with a psychologist and monthly ward rounds. Although the plan was moving towards decreasing components at the hospital, these components remained significant in breaking the cycle of admissions and enforcing the authority of section 3. If leave lasts longer than seven days, the RC must consider the use of community treatment orders (CTOs). However, they are not compelled to choose this option.

The impact of these judgements is that nurses may well be involved in the care of patients in the community who remain for some considerable time under the provisions of section 3. During that time such patients may be subject to further conditions or have their leave revoked and will continue to come under the treatment provisions of Part IV.

Revoking leave when the patient is outside the hospital

In order for an RC to revoke a patient's leave and recall them to hospital it must appear to them necessary to do so in the interests of the patient's health, safety or the protection of others, and they must inform the patient in writing. Except in emergency situations the recall should be based on current medical evidence that they remain mentally disordered (*Kay* v. *United Kingdom* [1998]). The Code of Practice paragraph 21.31 states that a refusal to take medication would not in itself justify recall, but would be a reason to consider it, and that when doing so the RC should consider the impact of recall on the patient (Welsh Code of Practice 28.29). The Code states that there is a duty to explain fully to the patient the reasons for recall and to record this in the patient's notes.

Medical treatment whilst on leave

Whilst on leave a patient remains under the Part IV treatment provisions that were explained in Chapter 5, and as such may in certain circumstances be given treatment for their mental disorder without consent. The Code of Practice states that if it is necessary to give the treatment without consent, then consideration should be given to recalling the patient to hospital but that such recall is not a legal requirement (Welsh Code of Practice 28.19). The Nursing and Midwifery Council (NMC) Code of Practice states that you are personally accountable for actions and omissions in your practice, and must always be able to justify your decisions. With this in mind and considering the issues raised in Chapter 5, nurses should resolve any concerns before proceeding with treatment in these circumstances.

Role of section 117 and care planning

For longer term periods of leave, nurses are likely to be fully involved in Care Programme Approach planning processes or equivalent. This should include consultation with all those involved and ensure all parties are aware of who to contact in the event of concerns.

If a patient is discharged from hospital on section 17 leave under a longer term section then they are entitled to section 117 aftercare, which places additional duties in relation to care planning and the provision of services. It places joint responsibility on the local authority and National Health Service (NHS) commissioning organisation to ensure that they provide aftercare services. These services can be provided in partnership with other organisations, are services that arise from an assessed need related to a person's mental disorder and their purpose is to reduce the risk of readmission to hospital. The Code of Practice states that they include meeting the patient's immediate needs for health and social care support and should aim to support them in regaining or enhancing their skills, or learning new skills, in order to cope with life outside hospital (Code of Practice 27.5; Welsh Code of Practice 31.7).

The Code of Practice states that the RC should ensure that the patient's needs for aftercare have been fully assessed, discussed with them and addressed in their care plan before the patient is discharged (para. 27.10). It gives guidance on what should be considered at paragraph 27.13. In order to achieve this they will need to be considered from early on in their admission. In practice it is likely to be nursing staff that do much of the co-ordination of this plan and identify many of the issues to be considered through their daily involvement with the patient.

Section summary

This section has explored how the powers connected to section 17 leave can be lawfully used by the RC to manage the transition from hospital to community and explored some of the challenges this raises for nurses. The duties created by section 117 in planning discharge from hospital have also been explained.

Absence without leave

There are times in which patients may be outside the hospital without this being authorised. This is always a significant issue but how significant it is can vary depending on the circumstances. For example, a patient having returned from leave a few minutes late is likely to be less serious than a patient absconding from a secure ward. The CQC states:

> It would be a mistake to view all such incidences as in some way reflecting poorly on the detaining authority involved, or indeed to draw any generalised conclusion from them: it is in the nature of positive risk taking that boundaries may, at times, be overstepped.
> (CQC, 2011, p59)

However, those involved in the patient's care will need to assess the risks, including the implication for future leave. For example, the Manchester University study 'Avoidable Deaths' found that 27 per cent of inpatient suicides occurred when the patient left the ward without asking permission.

In relation to section 17 leave, absent without leave (AWOL) patients are those who: have left the hospital in which they are detained without section 17 leave; have failed to return to the hospital at the time required to do so by the conditions of leave; are absent without permission from a place where they are required to reside as a condition of leave; or have failed to return to the hospital when their leave has been revoked (Code of Practice 22.2; Welsh Code of Practice 29.5).

Hospitals should have policies in place that detail who is to be informed, and who is responsible for seeking the return of the patient to the hospital. In this regard the Code states that the police should be asked to assist in returning a patient only when necessary and that where the patient's whereabouts is known their role should be to assist a suitably qualified and experienced mental health professional to return the patient (Code of Practice 22.13). However, if the patient is considered to be particularly vulnerable, dangerous, a restricted patient under Part III or a patient's history makes it desirable to inform the police the Code states the police should be informed immediately such a patient is missing.

The Act gives the power to take an AWOL patient into custody and return them to the detaining hospital to an approved mental health professional (AMHP), a member of the hospital staff, a police officer or a person authorised in writing by the detaining organisation. If the patient is on leave at another hospital then they may also be taken into custody by a member of staff of that hospital or a person authorised by that organisation.

The Code states that the arrangements for the safe return of the patient remain the responsibility of the detaining hospital. Exactly what happens in practice will depend on local agreements but nursing staff are likely, at some stage, to find themselves involved in planning and/or carrying out these arrangements. This may include the application for a warrant under section 135(2) at the magistrates' court. This is discussed further in Chapter 8.

When a patient goes AWOL the Code states that such instances should be reviewed and analysed so that lessons can be learned, including identifying patients most at risk of going AWOL. It is important that this information is accurately recorded as it can be used to identify many significant factors at a ward level that may be contributing to instances of AWOL. For example security issues on locked wards.

The Code also states that incidents of AWOL should be recorded in patients' notes and that if a patient has gone AWOL before this could include actions to be taken if the patient were to go missing again. For example, places they may have gone to, contact numbers or people to inform. Enabling a patient to discuss the reasons behind their actions may also identify factors that can be addressed to prevent it happening again and aid risk assessment.

> **Research summary: National Mental Health Development Unit:**
> *Strategies to Reduce Missing Patients: A practical workbook*
>
> This research explored the key reasons why patients go missing from mental health wards and suggested strategies to reduce the risk. The key factors included: being newly admitted or being in an acute period of their illness; a need to undertake essential tasks of daily living; dis-satisfaction with the ward environment, activities or care, as a response to receiving bad news; and insufficient security to prevent absconding. The strategies suggested to reduce the risks included reporting incidents and investigating them to promote understanding of the problem, developing entry and exit policies, providing meaningful engagement, structuring the day and having policies agreed with other organisations, particularly the police, about how any absence will be managed.

Urgent and emergency situations

Situations may arise in which a patient needs urgent leave but none has been granted. For example, their physical health deteriorates and they need emergency transfer to a general hospital. Such situations could be avoided by the RC authorising leave to acute hospitals in urgent situations. If this is not routinely done then nurses could raise the issue if it is a known risk in specific cases.

If this step has not been taken, nurses should be aware of the processes the organisation have put in place to fulfil their responsibility to ensure that whenever the normal RC is not available an approved clinician (AC) is available to step in and act as the RC when necessary. This person, as the RC, could authorise any such leave. This could be over the phone. In exceptional circumstances in which neither of these methods is available to the staff members, Richard Jones in the *Mental Health Act Manual* (2010, p119) states that the Mental Capacity Act 2005 or the patient's consent could be relied on to transfer them but the RC should grant the leave at the earliest opportunity as the patient is technically AWOL. Whatever route is followed nurses would be advised to request the normal RC to review arrangements at the earliest opportunity.

'Leave' for informal patients

> **Case study:** *Rabone v. Pennine Care NHS Foundation Trust* [2012] UKSC 2 [2012] MHLO 6
>
> *Melanie Rabone was admitted as an informal patient to a psychiatric hospital after attempting suicide. Whilst on a two day period of leave home she hanged herself. The hospital admitted that the decision to allow her leave was made negligently. However, a question arose in courts as to the hospital's duties*

with regard to Article 2 (Right to Life). The Supreme Court took the view that, when considering an organisation's duties under Article 2, informal psychiatric patients are in a different position to general hospital patients and are closer to that of patients detained under the MHA. In particular, they are an especially vulnerable group, may often be cared for in restricted circumstances or under some degree of control by the hospital, their judgement to remain may be impaired by their mental health, their co-operation may be influenced by their knowledge of the detaining powers under the MHA and section 5 holding powers can be used to prevent them leaving the hospital. The consequence of this ruling is that where a hospital knows or should have known about a real and immediate risk of suicide to an informal psychiatric patient they have a duty to take reasonable steps to prevent it. When considering what amounts to reasonable steps the court considered Melanie's right to autonomy.

This judgement presents real challenges to organisations and nurses working in psychiatric units. On the one hand, informal patients' rights to autonomy must be upheld. On the other, measures need to be put in place to assess risks to self and take reasonable steps to prevent any such risks without in effect detaining the person. As noted earlier the Manchester University Research identified that 27 per cent of psychiatric inpatient suicides occurred when patients left the ward without permission.

Regarding leave and informal patients the Code of Practice states:

> *Patients who are not legally detained in hospital have the right to leave at any time. They cannot be required to ask permission to do so, but may be asked to inform staff when they wish to leave the ward.*
> (Code paragraph 21.36; Welsh Code of Practice 28.6)

You will need to be clear about your duty to assess risk in relation to informal patients' management of their own leave and suicide, work with the patient and others to reduce this risk and discuss any concerns with the doctor in charge of the patient's care. You will also need to be aware of the organisation's policies in relation to assessing risk when a patient informs you they wish to leave the ward. This includes circumstances in which you may need to consider the use of section 5. At the same time you will need to ensure that you are not carrying out these duties in a way that in effect is requiring the patient to ask your permission to leave the ward.

Chapter summary

In this chapter you have been introduced to the practical and ethical dilemmas associated with detained patients' time on the ward. The processes and requirements of the MHA, that support this decision making and the management of shorter and longer term leave, have been introduced and the role of the nurse clarified. Finally, some of the issues related to informal patients' time off the ward have been introduced and you should now be in a position to explore how these are managed in the organisation in which you work.

Activities: brief outline answers

Activity 6.1

In order for a detained person to recover and take control of their own life again they will need time to re-establish their daily routines and reconnect with their social networks. This may mean reconsidering many aspects of their life including hobbies, employment, housing and social activities. All of these will require time off the ward to develop them. This can involve anyone or service that is important to them and achieving their recovery. If a person has leave too early, for too long or without the right support they could risk relapse, absconding, risk to themselves or not being able to maintain their social networks. The risks should be identified through a clinical risk assessment and must include risk to others.

Activity 6.2

The Code of Practice contains the model answer. See references given in task.

Activity 6.3

What type of leave would be essential as a part of his recovery   You will need to plan this with James, clarifying his goals and assessing what his needs in the community are. You will also need to consider, with him, what support he may need to maintain his recovery. At an early stage this could be addressing immediate needs around ensuring accommodation is not lost or that finances are maintained. If James is ready, it could also include occupational activities to balance the frustration he may feel about being detained on the ward.

Examples of the place, purpose and times of this leave   This will need to be based on a good assessment of James's needs and goals. It should be individualised to what is important to him and achieving his recovery. It could be to visit family or friends, engage in activities he enjoys, or explore developing employment or occupational activities.

What risks may be associated with it, and what conditions and contingency plans could be put in place to manage the risks   This should be based on the clinical assessment of James's risks and his mental state. You should consider what risks James can manage himself, what risks he needs support to manage and what risks he is not yet ready to manage himself. For example, it may be that in the early days James is a risk of absconding without an escort or even with an escort. Plans could include who James contacts, strategies he uses to manage his own distress and/or who others contact.

Activity 6.4

In order to resume his life James will need to be discharged from the ward at some stage. Being discharged can bring the opportunity for James to take greater control of his life, be more autonomous and do more of the things that bring a sense of wellbeing. However, it may also be a time of some anxiety around the lower level of support or the greater risks of not being able to maintain the practices and habits that enabled James to recover.

Further reading

Care Quality Commission (2010) *Leave of Absence and Transfer under the Mental Health Act 1983.* Newcastle: Care Quality Commission

For information on the link between leave and transfer of a patient.

Department of Health (2008) *Reference Guide to the Mental Health Act 1983.* London: TSO

More detailed reading on the main provisions of the MHA.

Department of Health (2008) *Reference Guide to the Mental Health Act 1983.* London: TSO, Chapter 13.

Information on leave of patients to countries other than England and Wales.

Useful websites

http://www.cqc.org.uk

Care Quality Commission guidance on notes on section 17 leave and their annual report on their monitoring duties in regard to the MHA.

Multiple choice questions

1. Which staff members can grant section 17 leave to a patient?

    (a) Their key nurse
    (b) Their responsible clinician
    (c) Any doctor
    (d) Any person authorised by their responsible clinician

2. In order for a condition to be attached to section 17 leave it must be:

    (a) Ideal for the effective management of the patient
    (b) Set out within hospital policies
    (c) Agreed on by the doctor and nursing team
    (d) Necessary in the interests of the patient or the protection of others

3. Which of the following statements is correct?

    (a) A patient must be placed on a community treatment order after seven days section 17 leave
    (b) If a patient is not an inpatient they cannot be on a section 3
    (c) A patient is not entitled to section 117 aftercare until after their section 3 is discharged
    (d) A responsible clinician must consider a community treatment order if a patient has been on section 17 leave for longer than seven days

4. If a nurse is concerned that a patient's risks have changed and it is no longer safe to proceed with section 17 leave what should they do?

    (a) Allow the leave but let the responsible clinician know as soon as possible
    (b) Withhold the leave on medical grounds
    (c) Proceed with the leave but ensure their risk assessment is fully recorded
    (d) Nothing as only a responsible clinician can grant leave

Chapter 7
Supervised community treatment

NMC Standards for Pre-registration Nursing Education

This chapter will address the following competencies:

Domain 1: Professional values

1. All nurses must practise in a holistic, non-judgmental, caring and sensitive manner that avoids assumptions; supports social inclusion; recognises and respects individual choice; and acknowledges diversity. Where necessary, they must challenge inequality, discrimination and exclusion from access to care.

2.1. Mental health nurses must practise in a way that addresses the potential power imbalances between professionals and people experiencing mental health problems, including situations when compulsory measures are used, by helping people exercise their rights, upholding safeguards and ensuring minimal restrictions on their lives. They must have an in depth understanding of mental health legislation and how it relates to care and treatment of people with mental health problems.

Domain 2: Communication and interpersonal skills

5.1. Mental health nurses must use their personal qualities, experiences and interpersonal skills to develop and maintain therapeutic, recovery-focused relationships with people and therapeutic groups. They must be aware of their own mental health, and know when to share aspects of their own life to inspire hope while maintaining professional boundaries.

NMC Essential Skills Clusters

This chapter will address the following ESCs:

Cluster: Care, compassion and communication

1. As partners in the care process, people can trust a newly registered graduate nurse to provide collaborative care based on the highest standards, knowledge and competence.

By the second progression point

7. Uses professional support structures to learn from experience and make appropriate adjustments.

By the third progression point

12. Recognises and acts to overcome barriers in developing effective relationships with service users and carers

Cluster: Organisational aspects of care

9. People can trust the newly registered graduate nurse to treat them as partners and work with them to make a holistic and systematic assessment of their needs; to develop a personalised plan that is based on mutual understanding and respect for their individual situation promoting health and well-being, minimising risk of harm and promoting their safety at all times.

By the second progression point

5. Contributes to care based on an understanding of how the different stages of an illness or disability can impact on people and carers.

By the third progression point

12. In partnership with the person, their carers and their families, makes a holistic, person centred and systematic assessment of physical, emotional, psychological, social, cultural and spiritual needs, including risk, and together, develops a comprehensive personalised plan of nursing care.

Chapter aims

By the end of this chapter you will be able to:

- understand the key issues in the debate surrounding the implementation of community treatment orders (CTOs);
- identify the ethical dilemmas behind the use of compulsion in the community;
- understand the provisions of CTOs and your duties and powers in this respect;
- identify practical steps to develop your practice, through reflection on research and reviews of CTOs.

Introduction

In life we can make mistakes which sometimes have very negative consequences. These may be about where we live, or using dangerous substances or alcohol. However, providing we have the mental capacity to make decisions, and unless we have committed a criminal offence, coercion is not normally used by the state to force us to act differently. However, this is not the case for those subject to CTOs.

This chapter will briefly describe the background regarding the debate surrounding compulsion in the community, and will consider the ethical issues, the practical difficulties and the research surrounding its effectiveness. It will explain the provisions of CTOs in England and Wales. Finally it will give you the opportunity to reflect on your obligations as a nurse and identify practical steps to develop your practice.

Note: The Code of Practice uses the term Supervised Community Treatment to describe the CTO regime in its entirety. However, this term is not used in the Mental Health Act (MHA) itself. This chapter will use the term CTO, unless directly quoting the Code of Practice.

Background to CTOs

The Code of Practice states the purpose of CTOs is

> *to allow suitable patients to be safely treated in the community rather than under detention in hospital, and to provide a way to help prevent relapse and any harm – to the patient or to others – that this might cause. It is intended to help patients to maintain stable mental health outside hospital and to promote recovery.*
> (Code of Practice English paragraph 25.2; Welsh paragraph 30.3)

Before the 2007 amendments to the MHA were agreed upon, there was considerable debate about the ethical justifications, the effectiveness and the practicality of a regime that would allow compulsory treatment in the community. On the one hand a group of patients, described as revolving door patients, were identified as being admitted compulsorily to hospital, recovering and being discharged, but then to stop taking medication, relapse and need compulsory admission again. Concerns about the risk this posed to the public increased following a number of high profile homicides. On the other hand, service user groups campaigned for greater rights and different professional groups raised concerns about the safety and practicality of imposing treatment in the community and the effect any community compulsion would have on therapeutic relationships. At the heart of the debates lie three principles: not interfering with the autonomy of a person; promoting and increasing someone's life chances and opportunities and therefore increasing the scope of their autonomy; and protecting the public from the risk posed by those with mental disorder.

Research summary

In 2008 the Department of Health published the research review, *International Experiences of Using Community Treatment Orders* (Churchill, 2008). This included consideration of the use of CTOs across six countries. It concluded that the research is beset by conceptual, practical and methodological problems, the general quality of the empirical evidence is *poor* and *It is not possible to state whether CTOs are beneficial or harmful to patients.*

The analyses did suggest that sustained CTOs combined with intensive mental health services may increase treatment adherence and reduce the risk of negative outcomes such as relapse, violent behaviour, victimisation and arrest. In addition, that the number of previous admissions, number of admissions during the CTO period, perceived coercion and medication adherence may also be important influences on outcome. It identified that the two most salient factors associated with reduced recidivism and improved outcomes appeared to be intensive mental health treatment and enhanced monitoring for a sustained period of time.

The research concluded that CTOs may play a complex role in increasing levels of services, but it is not clear whether they are necessary to improve services, or that they play any role in improving outcomes (p191).

Further to this, in 2013 Oxford University published findings of a study assessing the effectiveness of CTOs by comparing outcomes over a year period between a group of CTO patients and another group placed on section 17 leave. The main measurement was readmission rates. The study concluded that there was no statistical evidence that compulsory treatment in the community reduces readmissions.

> *Despite a more than three-fold increase in time under initial supervised community care, the rate of readmission to hospital was not decreased by CTOs. Neither was the time to readmission decreased nor was there any significant difference in the number or duration of hospital admissions. We also recorded no differences in clinical or social outcomes.*
> (Burns et al., 2013, p5)

These research findings are very challenging when considering your duty to ensure decisions are evidence based and to advocate for the patient and address imbalances in power.

Activity 7.1   *Reflection*

Before going on to explore your duties as a nurse, it will be helpful to reflect on your own beliefs and attitudes about CTOs. Make a list of:

- what the positive outcomes of a CTO could be for a patient;
- what the negative outcomes for a patient could be;
- what factors you think would contribute to a CTO being effective and what factors could negatively affect this.

Keep these in mind as you read the rest of the chapter.

There is an outline answer at the end of the chapter.

Section summary

In this section we have explored the background debate before the introduction of CTOs, considered some of the ethical and practical dilemmas behind them and considered research related to their effectiveness.

CTO: the main provisions

Only patients who have been detained in hospital for treatment and are still under that detention can be placed on a CTO. Patients can be on section 17 leave at the time of being placed on a CTO. The criteria for a CTO are set out in section 17(A). The responsible clinician (RC) must be satisfied that:

(a) *the patient is suffering from mental disorder of a nature or degree which makes it appropriate for him to receive medical treatment;*

(b) *it is necessary for his health or safety or for the protection of other persons that he should receive such treatment;*

(c) *subject to his being liable to be recalled as mentioned in paragraph (d) below, such treatment can be provided without his continuing to be detained in a hospital;*

(d) *it is necessary that the RC should be able to exercise the power under section 17E(1) below to recall the patient to hospital; and*

(e) *appropriate medical treatment is available for him.*

When deciding this the RC shall

consider, having regard to the patient's history of mental disorder and any other relevant factors, what risk there would be of a deterioration of the patient's condition if he were not detained in a hospital (as a result, for example, of his refusing or neglecting to receive the medical treatment he requires for his mental disorder).

However, a relapsing history leading to compulsory admissions does not need to be demonstrated before a patient can be placed on a CTO. Therefore there is nothing, in the Act, preventing a CTO being made in respect of a patient after their first admission, providing the criteria are met.

An RC who decides these criteria are met can make the CTO providing an approved mental health professional (AMHP) agrees in writing and states it is appropriate to make the order. When the CTO is made the original section the person was detained under is not discharged but remains dormant in the background.

The CTO is initially for six months but can be renewed for a further six months and then yearly. In order for it to be renewed the RC must see the patient in the two months before renewal. Before renewing the CTO, the RC must consult another professional involved in the patient's care. They may then renew the CTO provided that they are satisfied the criteria are met and an AMHP states in writing that the criteria are met and it is appropriate to extend the order.

Think back to the criteria for section 3 in Chapter 4. What are the key differences between the criteria for section 3 and for a CTO?

There is an outline answer at the end of the chapter.

Case study: *CNWL NHS Foundation Trust v. H-JH* [2012] UKUT 210 (AAC)

Mrs H was 36 years old, married with one child. She had mental health difficulties for approximately 12 years; initially her diagnosis was schizo-affective disorder. At the time of her tribunal her diagnosis was paranoid schizophrenia. She had a history of detention, under section 2 and section 3, of recovering after receiving treatment, then being discharged, stopping treatment and relapsing. The tribunal considered the only significant risk was deterioration to her own health. At the time of the tribunal she had been on a CTO for approximately three years. The First Tier Tribunal accepted that she lacked insight, believing that she had been cured following an exorcism by a Catholic priest and that she would likely stop taking medication with a risk of relapse. However, they accepted that her husband would monitor her mental state and ask her to go to the doctor if she began to relapse. They also accepted that if her husband did this she would comply. They therefore held that the grounds for the CTO were not met and discharged it. The Trust appealed to the Upper Tribunal. The Upper Tribunal found that with regard to this aspect of their decision their application of the law was correct and the decision was upheld. With regard to the powers of the CTO the Upper Tribunal Judge stated,

In the scheme of the mental health legislation, that is the lightest of control. But it is still control and she is entitled to be free of it if the statutory conditions for it are not met. She may be a classic revolving door patient, but she is entitled to be free from control when the door is open outwards.

(para. 14)

This case study demonstrates that the choice to use coercion should never be taken lightly, even if it seems that it is a reduced level of coercion. The burden to justify its use is always on those exerting it and, in line with the least restriction principle, all non-coercive means for achieving the same end should be ruled out first.

Conditions

Each CTO has two mandatory conditions: that the patient make themselves available for examination by the RC for the purpose of the RC determining if the grounds for renewing the CTO are met and that the patient make themselves available for examination by a second opinion appointed doctor (SOAD) if the SOAD has been asked to consider giving a treatment certificate. These are mandatory because they are necessary for the CTO to function. For example, the RC needs to see the patient to renew the CTO and if a treatment certificate by a SOAD is necessary then the patient can only continue to receive treatment if one is in place. Breaching one of these conditions is grounds in itself to recall the patient to hospital. However, depending on the reason the condition had not been met and the other circumstances it may not be necessary to recall.

The RC may also set other conditions to the CTO, providing they are for the purpose of:

(a) ensuring that the patient receives medical treatment;
(b) preventing risk of harm to the patient's health or safety;
(c) protecting other persons.

The Code of Practice states that the conditions should:

> *be kept to a minimum number consistent with achieving their purpose; restrict the patient's liberty as little as possible while being consistent with achieving their purpose; have a clear rationale, linked to one or more of the purposes in paragraph 25.30 [the purposes listed above]; and be clearly and precisely expressed, so that the patient can readily understand what is expected.*
> (Code of Practice 25.33; Welsh Code of Practice 30.30)

> *They might cover matters such as where and when the patient is to receive treatment in the community; where the patient is to live; and avoidance of known risk factors or high-risk situations relevant to the patient's mental disorder.*
> (Code of Practice 25.34; Welsh Code of Practice 30.33)

When the CTO is first made, an AMHP must agree that any conditions are appropriate. However, at any time after a CTO is in force the RC may vary the conditions without any such agreement with an AMHP.

The CTO does not contain any powers to enforce these conditions. Furthermore, although an RC may take a breach of these conditions into account when considering recall, the breach of them alone is not enough to recall a patient. Similarly, the CTO does not override the patient's right to refuse medication in the community. It may be helpful for you to think of the conditions as the RC communicating their view to the patient:

- of the essentials the patient needs to do in order to remain well and maintain their life in the community;
- that they (the RC) believe that not following them is likely to lead the patient to deteriorate to the extent they need to be recalled;
- that non-compliance with the conditions will be taken into account by the RC when they consider if the patient needs to be recalled.

You will recall the patient James we read about in Chapter 6. Here we continue with his story.

> ### Scenario
>
> *James is being discharged onto a CTO and the RC is considering what conditions to set. The RC initially wants to set them around residence, taking medication and occupation. However, you point out that in James's case it is his motivation that will enable him to maintain his tenancy and that he has demonstrated a clear desire to engage in his own occupational activities. However, he does have times when he is disinclined to take medication. James reluctantly acknowledges this. You discuss with James what support he will need to continue to take the medication. He values your input and would like to see you fortnightly. He would also like to arrange his appointment at the depot clinic around his part-time employment. The RC proposes to only add a condition about medication and you agree a support plan with James to enable him to remain well in the community.*

In the majority of cases the goal should always be to work towards each patient being an informal patient in the community and the use of a CTO may not be justified. However, if it is used the Code of Practice places significant emphasis on the need to have clear, agreed and robust care planning that has as much as possible promoted the participation of the patient and offered them support to comply with any conditions (Code of Practice 25.35).

Recall

At some stage a patient on a CTO may need to be recalled to hospital. The patient's RC is the only person who can recall a patient to hospital. However, if the normal RC is not available then organisations will need to have processes in place to allow another approved clinician (AC) to temporarily step into their shoes. The RC recalls a patient by completing a CTO3 and serving it or arranging for it to be served on the patient. Before recalling a patient the RC must be satisfied that:

(a) the patient requires medical treatment in hospital for his mental disorder; and
(b) there would be a risk of harm to the health or safety of the patient or to other persons if the patient were not recalled to hospital for that purpose.

As stated the RC may take any non-compliance with conditions into account when deciding if the criteria for recall are met. There may be situations in which a person has complied with conditions but for some other reason has relapsed and needs to be recalled. For example, despite continuing to take mediation and meet the other conditions, a loss in their family, physical illness or other such event has triggered a relapse to the extent that the person needs to be recalled to hospital for treatment. The patient may also be recalled to a different hospital than the one responsible for managing the CTO.

....

: **Case study**
:
: *James is discharged onto a CTO. Initially things go well and James begins to return to a daily routine*
: *that he much enjoys. However, after several months James has an argument with his boss at work that*
: *affects him badly. Over a period of a month you share concerns with James's parents that he is becoming*
: *more thought disordered, paranoid and disengaging from his daily routine.*
:
: *You discuss your concerns with the RC who agrees that it appears James is relapsing. The RC feels that*
: *James may need to be recalled but wants to see if she can negotiate with James before doing so. The RC*
: *visits James with you. He is clearly thought disordered and appears to be talking about people being*
: *against him and there being no point. He states he won't take any more medication and just wants to*
: *be left alone. The RC is of the view that there is no alternative but to recall James and completes the*
: *CTO3. The RC informs James of this and serves the CTO3.*

....

Managing recall

In this example James invited you both into his accommodation, the RC was able to serve the
CTO3 by hand and James agreed to return to hospital. However, things do not always go as
smoothly as this. Depending on local policies you may be involved in managing recall, which
can often be more complicated. For example, the CTO does not include any power to force-
fully enter premises or enter without the permission of those lawfully able to give it. In such
circumstances the powers discussed in Chapter 8 will need to be considered. You may not be
able to find the patient in order to serve a CTO3. In these circumstances the Mental Health
(Hospital, Guardianship and Treatment) (England) Regulations 2008 (SI 2008/1184) set out
actions that can be taken to enable the CTO3 to be considered served, and these are outlined
in Table 7.1

Method of serving Form CTO3	Notice effective?
Form served by hand to the patient	Effective immediately
Deliver form by first class mail to address where patient is believed to be	Served on the second working day after posting (e.g. posted Friday effective from Tuesday)
Deliver form by hand to patient's usual or last known address. If appropriate, consider whether section 135(2) warrant should be sought	Notice deemed to be served after midnight on the day it was delivered. It does not matter whether it is a working day, a weekend or a holiday. It does not matter whether it is actually received by the patient or not

Table 7.1: Method of serving a CTO3 and its impact on when it is considered served.

Once a notice is served, the patient is considered to be absent without leave (AWOL) and can be taken into custody and returned to the hospital as outlined in Chapter 6.

Duties and powers in respect of recalled patients

Once a patient is admitted to hospital they can be detained there for up to 72 hours. During that period they come under Part IV of the Act and so can only be treated under certain circumstances. These are described in Chapter 5 and set out in Table 5.1. As stated earlier, the original section that the patient was detained under before placed on the CTO has been put on hold. The RC now has the 72 hour period to decide if the patient should be discharged from the CTO altogether (which would also discharge the underlying section), be allowed back into the community under the CTO, or to revoke the CTO while reinstating the original detaining section. The CTO can only be revoked if the RC considers the criteria for a section 3 are met and an AMHP states, in writing, that they agree with the view of the RC and it is appropriate to revoke the CTO. If the CTO is revoked the time limits for renewal start as if it were a new detention.

Can a CTO patient be admitted informally?

In the case study, James did not recognise his need for hospital treatment and objected to it and any treatment. However, at other times it may be that a patient on a CTO is able to recognise the care team's concerns and agrees to hospital admission, or may even recognise signs of relapse and request hospital admission. The Act does allow the patient to be admitted informally in these circumstances. If this occurred James would have remained on a CTO and have continued to be subject to its treatment provisions whilst an inpatient. However, the Act does not allow section 5 holding powers to be used in respect of such patients. If, for example, after the informal admission James objected to being an inpatient or attempted to leave then the only mechanism the MHA provides to prevent this is recall by serving a CTO3. It may seem strange to say that you are 'recalling' a patient to hospital who is already in hospital. However, the recall is about the person's legal status in hospital not just their presence there. This may create difficulties for you if a patient attempts to leave when the normal RC is not immediately available, particularly out of hours. It will be important that you familiarise yourself with the local policy of who to contact and how to manage these situations. In its post-legislative scrutiny of the amendments to the MHA, the Department of Health identified this as a possible area of further amendment.

Section summary

In this section we have looked in detail at the main provisions of a CTO, including the criteria, conditions, recall and revoking a CTO. We have identified your role as a nurse, in particular, in relation to the recall of a CTO patient, complications that can occur and the recalled patient's status whilst on the ward.

Research/inspection findings regarding CTOs

We have already seen that the use of CTOs is contentious and there is as yet no clear research finding demonstrating its effectiveness. However, the fact cannot be escaped that CTOs are being used.

Although it is difficult to make evidence based decisions in the current context, there are research and reports that identify areas of concern regarding CTOs and describe service users' experience. You can use these in a reflective way to develop your practice with patients under CTO.

Research/reviews

Both the Care Quality Commission (CQC) and the Mental Health Alliance have produced reports reviewing the implementation of CTOs. They each raise a number of concerns. What follows are the key elements in relation to your role as a nurse.

Wide use of CTOs

Both the Mental Health Alliance and the CQC were concerned CTOs were being used for a wider group of people than for which it was intended. Specifically, CTOs were being used when there is no history of repeated compulsory admissions. The greater than expected use of CTOs does raise questions as to whether their use is going beyond when they are the least restrictive alternative and if the threshold of the power of recall being 'necessary' is being interpreted too broadly. For example, the CQC warn against them being used as a routine practice in the discharge process, and the Mental Health Alliance express serious concern that they may be being used to discharge patients earlier to free up bed space or in the context of a lack of adequate community support.

Increase use of depot medication

The CQC were concerned that a lack of trust in the patient managing their own medication may lead to an increased use of depots, as this is easier for professionals to monitor. However, they noted, some patients would prefer to not be on a depot because they find having it given humiliating, do not like the side effects or wish to manage their own medication (CQC, 2010a).

Issues concerned with general practitioners managing medication

The CQC were concerned that if medication is being managed by the general practitioner (GP), the GP may not ensure that prescribing complies with what is authorised or the patient has access to specialist pharmacological monitoring of appropriate dosage, or to the monitoring recommended by the Royal College of Psychiatrists in cases of high dose medication. They were also concerned that patients reported not being able to talk through difficulties with medication and side effects and that they were not always getting the advice they needed (CQC, 2010a).

Clear care planning

Having sought the views of a number of RCs, the Mental Health Alliance were concerned that confusion in care planning can occur in situations in which there are different inpatient and community RCs, with negative effects for the patient.

Engagement, coercion and support

The CQC identified: the concerns of a number of professionals regarding the effect that recall would have on engagement; the coercion informal CTO patients may feel when consenting to their admission and any treatment and if this was to the extent to invalidate the consent; a lack of access to support for patients and carers being over relied on; and difficulties accessing independent mental health advocates (IMHA).

Misrepresentation of powers

The CQC identified that staff and patients did not always understand that there was no power to enforce the conditions of a CTO, that a patient on a CTO has the right to refuse medication whilst in the community and that breaking a condition, other than the two mandatory conditions, was not sufficient in itself to justify recall. In particular they were concerned that Trusts were not discharging their duty to properly inform patients of these issues.

Disproportionate use amongst ethnic groups

As you will read in Chapter 8, those from Black and Ethnic Minority groups are disproportionately detained under the MHA 1983. Both the CQC and the Mental Health Alliance express concerns that this pattern is repeated in the disproportionate use of CTOs.

The paradox of success

Concern has been expressed by the CQC as to the length of time a patient may be subject to CTOs. In their research, Dawson et al. (2003) described this feature as the paradox of success. For patients detained in hospital the success of the detaining order is, on the whole, more easily stated. That is, it leads to a patient's recovery and they no longer need to be detained in hospital. However, as a purpose of CTOs is to prevent relapse, it is more difficult to judge when this is achieved. For example, a paradoxical argument arises in which the more a person's recovery is sustained the stronger the argument for the CTO. The danger is that the question is not asked as to when the risk should be taken to trust the person to manage their own care.

Five key action areas

These points can be summarised into five key action areas:

1. Ensure patient involvement in the planning of the CTO is maximised and CTOs are only used when necessary and alternatives have been ruled out.
2. Ensure the care team are clear about the powers of a CTO and the patient is informed of their rights.
3. Ensure the patient has access to independent support and advocacy (solicitor and an IMHA).
4. Ensure effective services are available to maximise the positive outcome of a CTO and reduce the risk of it being used to make up for a lack of services.
5. Ensure the question as to when each specific CTO should be discharged is asked and regularly reviewed.

CTOs and your duty as a nurse

As a lead inpatient nurse or care co-ordinator for the patient, you are likely to have a key role in the planning and monitoring of a CTO and are likely to have discussions with the patient and those in their social network. Read the NMC Standards for Pre-registration Nursing Education at the start of the chapter again, and consider what these could mean in the context of working with a service user on a CTO.

Put together the requirements setting out your duty to use your skills to create a therapeutic relationship and work cooperatively with the patient in an open and honest way that promotes recovery, addresses any power imbalances and in the process appropriately advocates for the patient. Gilbert and Plant (2010) argue that the coercive nature of CTOs is a threat to the therapeutic relationship between nurse and patient and that nurses must be aware of the issues to limit the damage and overcome the dangers and barriers.

How then will you comply with these duties when working with patients under CTOs? The starting point has to be to acknowledge that your relationship with the patient occurs in a specific social context and that it will be affected by this. For example, you will be a part of a government organisation and care team that has considerable power over the patient in an area where research indicates that power is often misunderstood as being greater than it actually is. At the same time, you may experience a strong desire for the patient to recover and take the steps they need to stay well but experience that despite your skills and the statutory powers, you are powerless to prevent the patient making the same mistakes.

Scenario

You have been allocated to work with John. He has a diagnosis of schizophrenia and a history of relapsing and being admitted to hospital, following disengagement from treatment. He is under a CTO. From his file, you identify that his relapses have often caused him a lot of harm, including the loss of tenancies and breakdown in relationships. He is currently stable in the community. You have met John on a couple of occasions and like him. You want him to remain well. During the most recent visit you realise that John believes the CTO means he cannot refuse medication and if he does he will be readmitted immediately. After further discussion, you realise that John wishes to stop medication due to the effect it has on his sexual function but has been frightened to raise this for fear of being recalled to hospital. You have also spoken to his parents who are concerned about the effect of John's relapses and want you to continue to tell him he must take his medication.

Scenarios like this can provoke a number of conflicting emotions and desires in you and you will need to give yourself a chance to reflect on what your duty as a nurse practising under the MHA is. For example, John has the right to know the limits of CTO powers and this may mean accepting the risk that he will make what may seem to be unwise decisions. Fulfilling your duty will mean not giving in to the temptation to turn a blind eye to John's misunderstanding in the hope he will stay well. At the same time it may be that with the right support John could be enabled to remain on a medication and limit the impact on his sexual function. Finally, John's parents will often be the ones who recognise signs of relapse first and can be more significantly affected. It is therefore important not to dismiss their concerns and ensure they have ways to raise concerns of relapse. However, you will also need to recognise that their idea of John's best interest may not always be the same as John's idea of his best interest.

This situation highlights that your role is being defined by a number of duties and social factors and these will create limits as to how you can advocate for the patient, form therapeutic relationships or address power imbalances. It is important that you learn to reflect on your practice and identify these factors in specific situations and that you are open and honest with the patient and those in their social network about what your role enables you to do and when you may have to do something they will not like. It may often be the case that involving another person to advocate for the patient is more effective, can go some way to addressing the imbalance of the power you have over them and can allow you to concentrate on a more specific piece of work. For example, a solicitor or IMHA could advocate for him regarding a change of medication, whilst you facilitate more expert advice from a pharmacist or specialist mental health sexual health worker.

Activity 7.3   *Evidence based practice and research*

You have now had an opportunity to consider in more detail your duties with regard to working with detained patients. Read back through the issues raised by the CQC and Mental Health Alliance. Then under the five key summarised points make a list of practical things you could do as a nurse to ensure patient's rights are upheld, restrictions are proportionate and promoting recovery remains at the centre of care decisions.

There is an outline answer at the end of the chapter.

Chapter summary

In this chapter you have been introduced to the context in which the debate about the use of compulsory powers in the community emerged, the ethical and practical issues surrounding this and the research concerning the effectiveness of CTOs. You have learnt about the provisions of CTOs and your duties in this regard. You have considered the concerns that reviews of the use of CTOs have raised and the implications this has for your practice. You will also have begun to reflect on how your duties under the MHA 1983 and the social context in which you practice can limit your ability to advocate for a patient, create power imbalances and affect your ability to form therapeutic relationships. You will also have begun to understand the importance of addressing these issues in complying with your duty as a nurse.

Activities: brief outline answers

Activity 7.1

The patient may engage better with services, comply with medication, sustain a recovery and improve their life chances.

The relationship with the patient may break down due to an experience of coercion and this could lead to disengagement and an increase in risks and relapse. It could also lead to the patient experiencing a sense of powerlessness and humiliation.

A positive involvement in care planning, negotiation of conditions and sufficient resources to support the patient are more likely to lead to positive outcomes. Less patient involvement, greater levels of restriction and a lack of support are more likely to lead to negative outcomes.

Activity 7.2

For both, the patient must have a mental disorder of a nature or degree requiring treatment, the risk criteria must be met and appropriate treatment must be available. However, it must be necessary for a section 3 patient to receive such treatment in hospital, whereas a CTO patient can receive such treatment without being detained in hospital, providing the RC has the power of recall and the power of recall is necessary.

Activity 7.3

1. Ensure patient involvement in the planning of the CTO is maximised.

You may want to reflect on the best way to engage the patient in the Care Programme Approach (CPA) process and ensure their views and wishes are represented and given proper consideration. This could include someone working with the patient to reflect on their wishes, views and goals. You may also work with the RC and the patient to enable the patient to be involved in the negotiation of conditions and distinguish between what is necessary as opposed to what is desirable.

2. Ensure the care team are clear about the powers of a CTO and the patient is informed of their rights.

You may want to obtain the rights leaflets from the CQC and ensure each person has a copy of them. You may want to ensure the patient knows to ask an IMHA or solicitor key questions. You may also want to reflect on your own feelings and ensure you are not tempted to overlook misunderstandings.

3. Ensure the patient has access to independent support and advocacy (solicitor and an IMHA).

You may want to make sure you know how to facilitate this and revisit it at reviews. If you are on a ward, you may want to ensure posters explaining rights are visible.

4. Ensure effective services are available to maximise the positive outcome of a CTO and reduce the risk of it being used to make up for a lack of services.

You may want to ensure that a person's needs are appropriately assessed through the CPA process and their entitlement to section 117 identified. This may mean flagging up any unmet needs you are aware of. This could include access to psychological therapies, groups or other alternatives to medication.

5. Ensure the question as to when each specific CTO should be discharged is asked and regularly reviewed.

This could be part of the CPA review, you could address it in any tribunal reports or you could develop a specific care plan.

Further reading

Bowen, P (2007) *Blackstone's Guide to the Mental Health Act 2007*. Oxford: Oxford University Press.

Care Quality Commission (CQC) (2010) *Monitoring the use of the Mental Health Act in 2009/10*. http://www.cqc.org.uk/sites/default/files/media/documents/cqc_monitoring_the_use_of_the_mental_health_act_in_200910_main_report_tagged.pdf

Care Quality Commission (CQC) (2011) *Monitoring the Use of the Mental Health Act in 2010/11*. http://www.cqc.org.uk/sites/default/files/media/documents/cqc_mha_report_2011_main_final.pdf

Details of the CQC's concerns.

Fennell, P (2007) *Mental Health: The new law*. Wiltshire: Jordan.

An explanation of the provisions of CTOs and the background debates.

Useful websites

http://www.blackmentalhealth.org.uk

http://www.mind.org.uk

http://www.rethink.org

Useful patient advocacy sites.

http://www.herc.ox.ac.uk/research/octet

Oxford study of CTOs.

Multiple choice questions

1. Which of the following patients can be placed under a community treatment order?

   (a)   An informal patient in the community
   (b)   A patient detained under section 2
   (c)   A patient detained under section 3
   (d)   An informal patient in hospital

2. Regarding community treatment order patients, which of the following are correct?

   (a)   Force can be used to ensure they comply with conditions
   (b)   A patient with capacity to refuse can routinely be forced to accept medication
   (c)   The responsible clinician can recall them to hospital if they are in need of further treatment as a recalled patient due to risk to self or others
   (d)   Any ward doctor can revoke a recalled patient

3. How long can a recalled patient be detained in hospital for before being discharged back on a community treatment order, discharged completely or revoked?

   (a)   28 days
   (b)   6 hours
   (c)   72 hours
   (d)   6 months

4. Regarding community treatment order patients informally admitted to hospital, which of the following is true?

(a) They can be treated with medication the same as detained patients
(b) They must be recalled immediately to hospital
(c) They have no right to leave the hospital without the responsible clinician's permission
(d) They cannot be subject to section 5 holding powers

Chapter 8
Courts and police powers

NMC Standards for Pre-registration Nursing Education

This chapter will address the following competencies:

Domain 3: Nursing practice and decision-making

9. All nurses must be able to recognise when a person is at risk and in need of extra support and protection and take reasonable steps to protect them from abuse.
9.1. Mental health nurses must use recovery-focused approaches to care in situations that are potentially challenging, such as times of acute distress; when compulsory measures are used; and in forensic mental health settings. They must seek to maximise service user involvement and therapeutic engagement, using interventions that balance the need for safety with positive risk-taking.

Domain 4: Leadership, management and team working

Mental health nurses must contribute to the leadership, management and design of mental health services. They must work with service users, carers, other professionals and agencies to shape future services, aid recovery and challenge discrimination and inequality.

4.1. Mental health nurses must actively promote and participate in clinical supervision and reflection, within a values-based mental health framework, to explore how their values, beliefs and emotions affect their leadership, management and practice.

NMC Essential Skills Clusters

This chapter will address the following ESCs:

Cluster: Care, compassion and communication

1. As partners in the care process, people can trust a newly registered graduate nurse to provide collaborative care based on the highest standards, knowledge and competence.

By the first progression point

5. Is able to engage with people and build caring professional relationships.

(continued)

continued ...

Entry to the register

14. Uses professional support structures to develop self awareness, challenge own prejudices and enable professional relationships, so that care is delivered without compromise.

4. People can trust a newly qualified graduate nurse to engage with them and their family or carers within their cultural environments in an acceptant and anti-discriminatory manner free from harassment and exploitation.

By the first progression point

1. Demonstrates an understanding of how culture, religion, spiritual beliefs, gender and sexuality can impact on illness and disability.

2. Respects people's rights.

Entry to the register

5. Is acceptant of differing cultural traditions, beliefs, UK legal frameworks and professional ethics when planning care with people and their families and carers.

Cluster: Organisational aspects of care

9. People can trust the newly registered graduate nurse to treat them as partners and work with them to make a holistic and systematic assessment of their needs; to develop a personalised plan that is based on mutual understanding and respect for their individual situation promoting health and well-being, minimising risk of harm and promoting their safety at all times.

By the second progression point

9. Undertakes the assessment of physical, emotional, psychological, social, cultural and spiritual needs, including risk factors, by working with the person and records, shares and responds to clear indicators and signs.

By entry to the register

15. Works within the context of a multi-professional team and works collaboratively with other agencies when needed to enhance the care of people, communities and populations.

Chapter aims

By the end of this chapter you will be able to:

- understand the relationship between the criminal justice services and the mental health services;
- identify the various ways services from criminal justice can be involved in the admission of patients to a psychiatric hospital;
- understand the warrants that enable the police to gain access to private property to admit a person to a place of safety or return an absent without leave (AWOL) patient;

- understand the different security ratings of wards;
- consider the greater restrictions some patients are placed under and the duties nurses have towards them;
- begin to think about the implications of the disproportionate detention of those from Black and Ethnic Minority groups on the care provided by nurses.

Introduction

There are instances in which people with mental disorders are a risk to others and may commit crimes. However, the police can be involved when there has been no crime or risk to others, and we must remember that people formally admitted to psychiatric units are vulnerable individuals and are admitted, often under considerable restrictions, for the purpose of treatment or assessment, not punishment.

This chapter will briefly explain the relationship between the criminal justice system and mental health services and outline the main ways in which people can be admitted to hospital via the court or police routes. It will address the kinds of facilities in which such people may be cared for and will deal with particular restrictions on liberty that pertain to people transferred to hospital from prison/courts. Finally it will consider the implications on nurses of the disproportionate detention of those from Black and Ethnic Minority groups.

Links between the criminal justice system and mental health services

The police and wider criminal justice system cross over with mental health services in many different ways. It is important to recognise that some of the most common ways do not involve the person having committed an offence. For example, a police officer may, in the daily course of events, come across an individual they are concerned about and refer for specialist mental health services. In these instances it is important that the person concerned is not criminalised but receives the necessary health care support they need.

In other instances, in which a possible offence is involved, decisions have to be made in relation to a number of key principles:

- that justice is served by appropriately and fairly convicting a person of any offence, whilst taking into account how they may be less culpable for the offence due to their mental disorder;
- that the public are protected;
- that treating a mental disorder may reduce the risk of reoffending;
- that those with mental disorders are likely to be more vulnerable to self-harm, suicide or abuse whilst in custody and are in need of protection.

In April 2009 the Department of Health published *The Bradley Report: Lord Bradley's review of people with mental health problems or learning disabilities in the criminal justice system* (Bradley, 2009). Lord Bradley considered the complex link between mental disorder and offending and argued that services need to work together to make sound decisions about the correct form of intervention. This could involve a purely health intervention, a criminal justice-led intervention or a combination of both, depending on the specific circumstances of the case, including the nature of the offence and the relationship to the mental disorder. He argued that this assessment and decision making should start as early as possible on the 'offender pathway', and that there should be greater awareness of mental health and learning disability issues in front line community policing.

In particular, he stressed the need for mental health teams to be based in police stations and courts and that account should be taken of social exclusion issues and the specific challenges faced by women, those with difficulties in relation to alcohol or substances alongside mental health difficulties, those with learning disabilities and those from Black and Ethnic Minority groups. This approach has resulted in a wide range of interventions from purely informal healthcare in the community, civil detention in hospital, a criminal justice community order with a mental health treatment requirement, healthcare in prison, to a hospital order under the Mental Health Act (MHA). Two key concepts in his report were 'diversion' and 'offenders with mental health problems'.

Concept summary: diversion and offenders with mental health problems

'Diversion' is a process whereby people are assessed and their needs identified as early as possible in the offender pathway (including prevention and early intervention), thus informing subsequent decisions about where an individual is best placed to receive treatment, taking into account public safety, safety of the individual and punishment of an offence.
(Bradley, 2009)

Offenders with mental health problems:

Those who come into contact with the criminal justice system because they have committed, or are suspected of committing, a criminal offence, and who may be acutely or chronically mentally ill ... It also includes those in whom a degree of mental disturbance is recognised, even though it may not be severe enough to bring it within the criteria laid down by the Mental Health Act 1983.

Scenario

John is a 19 year old who left home following an argument with his parents. He has been sleeping on friends' couches for several months. He was arrested late on a Thursday night, in the city centre, for being drunk and disorderly. Later at the police station he began to tell an officer that he has a very low mood, has been self-harming and experiencing thoughts of hopelessness. The officer requests an assessment by the link mental health nurse. The nurse is able to assess John for his mental health needs, including depression and is also able to assess his social needs, link him with a general practitioner (GP) and arrange for him to attend the local homeless shelter for young people.

This chapter is concerned with the routes that could lead to a person receiving care and treatment in hospital and the nature of that care and treatment. However, it should be noted that mental health nurses regularly work within diversion services, with people subject to a Criminal Justice Act 2003 Community Order with a Mental Health Treatment Requirement or as a social supervisor of a conditionally discharged patient subject to a Home Office Restriction Order.

Police powers: sections 135 and 136

These powers do not relate to an offence but do involve police and are likely to lead to a hospital admission, even if that is only as the place of safety. Section 135 relates to warrants given by magistrates and has two parts: section 135(1) and section 135(2). Section 136 is a police power to remove a mentally disordered person found in a public place to a place of safety.

Section 135(1)

Section 135(1) is a warrant applied for by an approved mental health professional (AMHP) that allows a police officer, accompanied by a doctor and an AMHP to enter a premises, if need by force, where they believe a person suffering from a mental disorder is within. If thought fit, they will remove the person to a place of safety with a view to making an application for their detention or any other arrangements. When applying for the warrant the AMHP must satisfy the magistrate that the person:

(a) has been, or is being, ill-treated, neglected or kept otherwise than under proper control, in any place within the jurisdiction of the justice; or

(b) being unable to care for himself, is living alone in any such place.

The warrant is necessary when there is no other authority under which to enter a private premises.

Scenario

Peter is well known to mental health services and sees a nurse every three weeks. He has a diagnosis of bipolar disorder and is known to self-neglect and disengage when he is depressed. His friends and housing provider have recently contacted the community mental health team with concerns that Peter has not been going out and is refusing to answer when they call round to see him. He has not collected his medication in four weeks. The team attempts to call round on two occasions but Peter refuses to talk

(continued)

continued ...

> *to them. His curtains are drawn and it appears the lights are off. His nurse is concerned at the level of*
> *self-neglect, discusses the case with the consultant psychiatrist and refers it to the AMHP team. The*
> *AMHP attempts to visit with the psychiatrist and another doctor but Peter makes it clear that he does*
> *not want to speak to them and will not let them in. The AMHP therefore applies for a section 135(1)*
> *warrant and Peter is taken to and assessed at a place of safety.*

Section 136

Like section 135(1), section 136 gives a police officer the power to remove a person to a place of safety. The person must appear to the police officer to be suffering from a mental disorder, be in need of immediate care or control, be in a place to which the public have access and the police officer must think it necessary to remove them in their interests or for the protection of others. After being taken to a place of safety under section 135(1) or section 136 a person can be kept there for the purpose of assessment for no longer than 72 hours. The power to detain also ceases once any assessments are complete and necessary arrangements made or a doctor considers the person to not be mentally disordered.

Concept summary: place of safety

Section 135(6) defines a place of safety as

> *residential accommodation provided by a local social services authority under Part III of the*
> *National Assistance Act 1948, a hospital as defined by this Act, a police station, an independ-*
> *ent hospital or care home for mentally disordered persons or any other suitable place the occupier*
> *of which is willing temporarily to receive the patient.*

The Code of Practice requires organisations to establish local policies setting out the places of safety that are to be used in their area. As identified above persons held in a place of safety are not there because they have committed a criminal offence and those with mental disorders can be more vulnerable to committing self-harm or suicide if in police custody. Both the Welsh and English Codes stress that a police station should only be used as a last resort, due to the risk posed to others. The preferred place of safety should be the one within a suitable hospital.

If the place of safety is a hospital then you may, in your role as a nurse, receive a person into it and be responsible for their care whilst they are there. It will be important that you know the local policies that set out how your duties to the patient are met. In particular, that they receive any medical treatment or assessment, they are informed of their rights, and access to legal advice is facilitated if requested by them. There are no provisions within the MHA to treat a patient detained at a place of safety under section 135(1) or section 136 without their consent. It is therefore essential that if administering treatment you seek the patient's consent or consider the provisions of the Mental Capacity Act 2005 if they lack capacity to consent. The MHA allows patients to be transferred between places of safety. If the patient is transferred to a hospital place of safety in which you have responsibilities it will be important that you are clear about the time they were detained at the first place of safety, as this is the time from which the 72 hours starts.

Section 135(2)

In the context of

- patients already detained but who have absconded,
- recalled patients under community treatment orders (CTOs) that have failed to return to hospital, or
- CTO patients who have absconded after having been admitted to hospital under recall,

section 135(2) is a warrant that authorises a police officer to enter a premises in which there is reasonable cause to believe that person is and admission to the premises has been refused or that such refusal is apprehended and to remove that person to where they are required to be at. The warrant can be applied for by a police officer, AMHP, officer of the staff of the hospital in which the person is liable to be detained or any other person authorised to do so by the detaining authority. There should be local policies in place that set out who should apply for the warrant in which circumstances.

Although the warrant only gives a police officer the power to enter and remove the person, it should be recognised that police officers are not expert in mental health and it would normally be good practice for them to be accompanied by a mental health professional, if possible someone who knows the patient and the most effective way to communicate with them. The Welsh Code of Practice goes as far as stating that it is good practice that the patient's responsible clinician (RC) accompanies the police officer (Code of Practice 7.4). The English Code of Practice states it should be a person authorised by the detaining hospital or, in the case of a CTO patient, a member of their care team.

As discussed a person who is taken into custody under the authority of section 135 or section 136 has not committed a criminal offence but is in need of assessment and/or treatment. Attempts should therefore be made not to criminalise the process. In particular, the English and Welsh Codes of Practice state that there should be local multi-agency policies in place that set out the processes around conveyance and that the method used should be the one most consistent with managing the person's dignity and privacy whilst being consistent with managing the risks. Both Codes stress that a police vehicle should not be the normal means of conveyance. Other alternatives could be via an ambulance, with or without the police.

Scenario

James is currently on a CTO and you are his community care co-ordinator. His RC has served the CTO3 and he is now recalled. However, he is refusing to return or allow anyone in his house. The appropriate warrant has been obtained and James's recall co-ordinated with the hospital ward, police and ambulance services.

If involved in such situations, you will need to consider the implications of your duty to *make the care of people your first concern, treating them as individuals and respecting their dignity* alongside your duty to *work with others to protect and promote the health and wellbeing of those in your care, their families and carers, and the wider community* (NMC, 2008, p2).

It touches many of the standards required to be met for pre-registration nursing, including working in a multidisciplinary team to undertake sound assessments, manage risk and preserve dignity.

Activity 8.1   *Decision thinking*

Consider James's situation and answer the following questions.

- What warrant should have been sought?
- Who could apply for it?
- What factors should be considered in planning James's admission?
- Who can convey James?

There is an outline answer at the end of the chapter.

Section summary

In this section we have considered the various routes by which patients who have not committed an offence may be admitted to hospital with police involvement. In doing so we have explored how you may be involved as a nurse and what factors need to be taken into account when managing situations to respect the dignity of the service user, whilst ensuring the safety of those involved.

Admission of those suspected or convicted of offences

The MHA 1983 establishes powers for the courts to detain those suspected or convicted of an offence at different stages in the criminal justice pathway including before sentencing, at sentencing and after a person has been sentenced to prison. The key features of these powers are summarised below. In all cases the courts cannot make such orders unless the approved clinician (AC) in overall charge of the person's care or the organisation that would be the detaining organisation have made provisions for the person's admission.

Before sentencing

At any time before sentencing certain courts can, under section 35 or section 36, remand a person accused of an offence punishable by imprisonment to hospital. If this power is used the person must be admitted to the hospital within seven days. The remand is initially for 28 days but the court may extend this by a further two 28 day periods. If the person absconds at any stage they may be brought back before the court. The court can end the remand at any time. A person remanded to hospital cannot be given section 17 leave or transferred to another hospital.

Section 35 is for the purpose of providing the court with a report and can be used by magistrate and Crown courts. The criteria that have to be met are that there is reason to suspect the person is suffering from a mental disorder and it would not be practicable for the report to be done if the person was bailed. The MHA does not provide any powers to treat those under section 35 without the consent of the patient. The report must be prepared by an AC. This could be a nurse. The reports normally contain whether the person is suffering from a mental disorder, its link to the offence, other significant factors and recommendations on care and treatment.

Concept summary

The link between an offence and a person's mental disorder can be complex and involve a number of other factors. In his report Lord Bradley refers to a summary of the relationship submitted to him by the Royal College of Psychiatrists.

The anti-social behaviour is directly related to or driven by aspects of mental disorder. In this case, effective treatment of the mental disorder would be likely to reduce the risk of further anti-social behaviour.

The anti-social behaviour is indirectly related to mental disorder.

Treatment would be likely to make a contribution to a reduction in offending but would not be sufficient in itself to tackle offending behaviour.

The anti-social behaviour and the mental disorder are related by some common antecedent, for example childhood abuse.

Treatment of the mental disorder in itself would not be sufficient to tackle re-offending.

The anti-social behaviour and the mental disorder are coincidental.

The mental behaviour is at least partly secondary to the anti-social behaviour.
(Extract from the submission to the review by the Forensic Faculty,
Royal College of Psychiatrists, 6 March 2008)

Understanding the relationship between the offence and a mental health difficulty is important in deciding the most appropriate way to intervene when seeking to ensure there is a just outcome, seek a balance with preventative intervention and reduce risk of reoffending.

Section 36 enables a Crown court to remand a relevant person to hospital for a period of treatment. Its purpose is that following the treatment the person who was not fit for trial may become fit. The court needs the evidence of two doctors that the person is suffering from a mental disorder of a nature or degree which makes him appropriate to be detained in hospital for medical treatment and appropriate medical treatment is available for them. A person accused of murder cannot be remanded under section 36.

If a person who has not yet been sentenced is initially remanded to prison and then becomes mentally unwell, the Secretary of State may, under section 48, direct that they be removed to hospital providing that there are two medical reports stating that:

(a) the person is suffering from mental disorder of a nature or degree which makes it appropriate for him to be detained in a hospital for medical treatment; and
(b) he is in urgent need of such treatment; and
(c) appropriate medical treatment is available for him.

Such a person would come under the Part IV treatment provisions, as discussed in Chapter 5, and would be subject to a restriction order.

Admission to hospital at the point of sentencing

If a person is convicted of an offence punishable by imprisonment then a Crown court or magistrates' court may make a hospital order in place of a penal punishment. There does not have to be a link established between the mental disorder and the offence, and a hospital order is not a punishment; its sole purpose is to ensure the person receives the care and treatment they need. In order to make a hospital order under section 37 the courts must have reports from two doctors stating that the person is suffering from a mental disorder, is of a nature or degree which makes it appropriate for him to be detained in a hospital for medical treatment and appropriate medical treatment is available for him. If the person who would be the RC is unsure if the person would respond to the treatment then the court may make an interim hospital order to enable this to be assessed. An interim hospital order is initially for 12 weeks and may be renewed at 28 day intervals up to a maximum of 12 months.

Before making a section 37 order the court must also be satisfied that

> *having regard to all the circumstances including the nature of the offence and the character and antecedents of the offender, and to the other available methods of dealing with him, that the most suitable method of disposing of the case is by means of an order under this section.*
> (s37(2)(b))

Section 37 cannot be used for a person convicted of murder. This enables those making the decision to take into account the issues that are relevant in the particular circumstances and gives them a lot of discretion. The issues will include the seriousness of exactly what the person did, how their mental health difficulties were and are affecting them, what hospital treatment could realistically achieve, the likely impact of alternatives, such as a custodial sentence, the best way for any significant risks to be managed and reduced and the relationship between the offence and the mental disorder. It is worth bearing in mind that the court will consider not just the health needs of the person but also the need to punish certain serious offences. For example, the less the link between the offence and the mental disorder and the more culpable the person, the more weight may be given to the need to punish a serious offence.

A patient detained under section 37 may or may not be subject to a restriction order. If there is no restriction order then they are in the same position as a patient detained under section 3 apart from the fact that they cannot apply for a tribunal within the first six months and their nearest relative cannot apply for their discharge.

Only a Crown court may make a restriction order. This is often written as a section 37/41 patient. However, if a magistrates' court believes the ground for one is met they may refer the case to the Crown court, providing the person concerned is over 14 years of age. The Crown court must be satisfied that the restriction order is necessary for the protection of the public from serious harm. In considering this they must have regard to the nature of the offence, the antecedents of the offender and the risk of his committing further offences if set at large. The effect of a restricted hospital order is that:

- the person's detention does not have to be renewed;
- the person cannot be transferred, granted leave or discharged by the RC unless the Mental Health Unit in the Ministry of Justice agree;
- the person cannot be discharged by the hospital managers unless the Mental Health Unit in the Ministry of Justice agree;
- the person may be conditionally discharged from hospital (discharged subject to conditions set by the Ministry of Justice and subject to recall); and
- a tribunal may absolutely or conditionally discharge a patient and they may apply once in every year.

A restriction order may be discharged by the Mental Health Unit in the Ministry of Justice, who undertake this role on behalf of the Secretary of State.

Section 45A gives the Crown court the power to make what has been described as a 'hybrid order'. In effect the person is given a prison sentence but initially detained in hospital. If the person is successfully treated before the prison sentence expires they can then be sent to prison if the RC recommends it and the Secretary of State grants a warrant. If their prison sentence ends, the hospital direction component continues until discharged. The person is automatically made subject to restrictions as described above.

Transfer from prison

Once a person has been sentenced to prison they may be transferred to hospital under section 47 by warrant of the Secretary of State. The Secretary of State must be satisfied by reports from two medical practitioners that the person is suffering from a mental disorder of a nature or degree which makes it appropriate for him to be detained in a hospital for medical treatment and that appropriate medical treatment is available for him. The Secretary of State must also be satisfied, having regard to the public interest and all the circumstances, that it is expedient for the transfer to occur.

The Department of Health (2011) has issued guidance on the use of both section 47 and section 48.

The transfer direction may have restrictions imposed as discussed above. These can also name the specific ward in which the person must be detained. The restrictions allow the person to be transferred back to prison if they are successfully treated but expire when the prison sentence ends. If the restrictions do expire then the person is in the same position as a section 37 patient without restrictions.

Activity 8.2   *Critical thinking*

Transfers and remands to hospital are not punishments but are for the purpose of assessment or treatment. This is reflected by the fact that the criteria have much in common with civil sections. For example, the medical component of the sections concerning treatment is based on a three part test. Look back over the civil sections, as outlined in Chapter 4, and the sections above and see if you can identify the three parts.

There is an outline answer at the end of the chapter.

Section summary

This section has explored how those subject to criminal proceedings may be admitted to hospital at different stages of those proceedings. We have emphasised the importance of remembering that those transferred are transferred for assessment or treatment and not punishment. We have also explored the rights of these patients and some of the implications for nurses working with them.

Caring for people in different forms of secure facility (low secure, medium secure, high secure)

Patients detained under Part III and civil patients may be detained in the same hospital environments. It is therefore important not to make assumptions about where patients are just because of the section they are under. These decisions should be made based on an assessment of the individual patient, particularly the risks. For those patients who need to be in more secure units there are three categories: low, medium and high.

Concept summary: low, medium and high security units

Low security units are defined in *Mental Health Policy Implementation Guide: National minimum standards for general adult services in psychiatric intensive care units (PICU) and low secure environments* (Pereira and Clinton, 2002). They are for patients who exhibit disturbed behaviour in the context of a mental disorder and who need a degree of security to manage them. They seek to balance the need for security with the need for the environment to be homely, integrated with the community and to promote recovery. The guidance suggests a patient can stay for up to two years.

Medium security services are provided by a range of National Health Service (NHS) and independent sector organisations, and are for people who present a significant danger. Many patients will have a history of offending and some will have been transferred from prison or from court to receive inpatient treatment. Typically, patients will remain in treatment for between two and five years.

High security services are provided at Ashworth, Broadmoor and Rampton hospitals; each hospital is part of an NHS Trust. At present, the Department of Health's relationship with high security hospitals is different from that with any other NHS service, as the National Health Service Act 2006 places a specific duty on the Secretary of State for Health to provide high security hospital services. Patients in high security hospitals present a grave and immediate danger to the public and require a significant period of treatment.

Case study: *Munjaz* v. *UK* 2913/06 [2012] MHLO 79 (ECHR)

Munjaz was detained in a high security hospital. Whilst there he was subject to a seclusion regime that departed from and was more restrictive than the guidelines in the Code of Practice. He argued that this violated his Article 8 rights due to the impact it had on his opportunities for developing relationships with others and his personal development. Although the court held that the actions of the hospital were sufficiently justified and scrutiny of them sufficiently robust, so there was no violation of Article 8, they did establish the principle that has been described as residual privacy. In essence, any restrictions on a person already deprived of their liberty that interfere with Article 8 must also comply with Article 8. What this means was more clearly set out in a case before the Court of Protection: J Council *v.* GU & Ors *[2012] EWHC 3531 (COP). This case is outlined below.*

GU suffered from a number of separable mental disorders, viz. childhood autism, obsessive–compulsive disorder, dissocial personality disorder, mixed anxiety disorder and paedophilia. In order to manage risk to children he had significant restrictions placed on his contact with others, his access to post, his

(continued)

continued ...

telephone contact, his personal space and he was searched. It was clear he was deprived of his liberty and this was authorised via a Deprivation of Liberty Safeguards (DOLS) authorisation. However, unlike the MHA that has clear guidance and legislation regarding further restrictions on those detained, the DOLS scheme has no such guidance. The judge held that to be compliant with Article 8 these further restrictions needed to be based in some form of legal provision, for example the MHA Code of Practice, have to be accessible to the person, be predictable and the scope of the authority of those exercising the powers must be clearly set out to prevent their arbitrary use.

In their reports, *Monitoring the Mental Health Act 2009/10* and *2010/11* (CQC, 2010a, 2012), the Care Quality Commission (CQC) raised a number of concerns regarding the restrictions on detained patients including: blanket ward rules that restricted access to leave, personal items and the choice to smoke, the overuse of restraint and seclusion that did not comply with the Code of Practice and instances in which seclusion and long term segregation were being used but not recognised as such. They recommended that the restrictions patients were subject to could be reduced by improving ward environments through therapeutic activities, and ensuring restrictions are based on individual risk assessments and comply with the Code of Practice. In particular the report stresses the requirement of the Code to ensure patients are given the opportunity to reflect on instances of seclusion or restraint and record their views.

A further example of restrictions on patients is section 134 which sets out the circumstances in which a person's outgoing post can be withheld and circumstances in which incoming post can be withheld from those in high secure hospitals. This includes the patient's right to request a decision to withhold incoming post be reviewed by the CQC or Welsh ministers. The MHA Code of Practice sets out further requirements in relation to: seclusion, long term segregation, restraint and physical interventions, the use of mechanical restraint, observation, searching patients, use of mobile phones and internet access, and visits to patients. The majority of these require organisations to have policies in place. Finally, the Code requires units with enhanced levels of security to have policies setting out the categories of patients for whom it is appropriate to use physically secure conditions and those for whom it is not appropriate.

It is not within the scope of this chapter to cover each of these in detail. However, in order to comply with the requirements of the Nursing and Midwifery Council (NMC) Code of Conduct and your pre-registration nursing requirements it is essential that you are aware of the policies covering these restrictions in the areas in which you work. For example, consider the implications of the pre-registration nursing requirements referred to at the start of the chapter and the NMC Code of Conduct requirements in relation to promoting trust and working collaboratively.

It is worth remembering that those detained and then subject to further restrictions are in a particularly vulnerable position and have a considerable degree of power exercised over them. They are also in hospital for the purpose of treatment or assessment and not punishment. You have a key role in ensuring that their human rights are not breached and that any work with them can be for the purpose of a positive recovery. Furthermore, the pre-registration standards you are required to meet and maintain focus on promoting choice and participation and interventions being based on evidence based person-centred assessments and risk assessments.

Case study

Martin is a patient in a low security unit. He is detained under section 37 with restrictions. He has a diagnosis of paranoid schizophrenia. He has been recently recalled to hospital. He is angry after being recalled. He has been allowed access to his mobile phone but has recently had it taken from him after he was using it to take pictures of other vulnerable inpatients and to send sexually explicit messages to the sister of another inpatient. He obtained her number by looking at the other inpatient's phone without permission.

Activity 8.3　　　　　　　　　　　　　　　　*Critical thinking*

Article 8 refers to restrictions being based in law, foreseeable, the decision making around them being accessible to the person concerned and the scope of the powers being clear. It is important that these rights are real and not just hypothetical and, in ensuring this, that you consider your wider duties as a nurse. Consider Martin's case and answer the following questions.

- What sections of the English and Welsh Code of Practice are relevant to this situation?
- How are the guiding principles relevant?
- How could you limit the impact of any intervention?
- Who else may be able to assist the patient to understand the provisions around removing the mobile phone and advocate for them?

There is an outline answer at the end of the chapter.

Section summary

This section has considered wards of different levels of security and the implications for patients treated and assessed on these wards. It has been stressed that the choice of ward a person is admitted to should be based on clinical assessment of risk and not just what section they are under. Similarly, further restrictions on patients should be based on individual risk assessments and not blanket decisions. Finally, the importance of placing these further restrictions under added scrutiny, not less, has been emphasised.

Black and Ethnic Minority groups

A key nursing leadership duty is to work for the development of services that address inequality and improve patient outcomes. A starting point has to be an acknowledgement of the inequalities and unequal power relationships that exist within social relations. In the context of working with those under Part III of the MHA and those in secure settings, that means recognising the degree of power the care team has over them and the inequalities that already exist in relation to specific social groups.

The 'Count me in' census looked at the detention rates by ethnic groups. It was a five year project starting in 2005 and collected and analysed statistics on one day of each year. Some of the key findings were that the higher detention rates of those from certain Black and Ethnic Minority communities or groups was statistically significant, as was the use of Part III of the MHA for these groups. Furthermore, referrals for these groups were more likely to come from the criminal justice system. For example in the 2010 census,

> *Of all patients detained on admission, 14% were detained under section 37 with a section 41 restriction order applied … In all minority ethnic groups, very few women were detained under section 37/41. Among men, the rate of detention for the White British group was 16% lower than average, and it was higher than average in the White/Black Caribbean Mixed group by 77%, the Black Caribbean group by 100%, the Black African group by 27% and the Other Black group by 52%.*
> (Care Quality Commission and National Mental Health
> Development Unit, 2010)

A consistent pattern across all six annual censuses was the higher than average detention rate under section 37/41 for the Black Caribbean and Other Black groups.

This work occurred alongside the Delivering Race Equality project, which is now being replaced by New Horizons. It will be important that you consider any issues in relation to the impact of race, or other such individual characteristics, in your care planning and that you are familiar with the research in relation to your area of practice.

Section summary

This section has highlighted the disproportionate detention of those from Black and Ethnic Minority groups and the implications for nurses' duties to address imbalance in power relationships and develop services that promote equality. This is a challenging area and one you may wish to explore further.

Chapter summary

This chapter has considered the various ways that those involved with the criminal justice services can be admitted to hospital. It is important to recognise that in many situations the person admitted to hospital will not have committed an offence and should not be criminalised.

Furthermore, even when the person is alleged to have committed an offence or has been convicted of an offence, they are admitted to hospital for treatment or assessment and not punishment. Those detained in hospital are a vulnerable group and even more so when they are exposed to further restrictions on their autonomy. We have considered the patients' human rights, the requirements of the MHA and the wider nursing duties and stressed the need to ensure that any further restriction is subject to further scrutiny and not less, in particular that it complies with the requirements of the Code of Practice and is based on individualised risk assessment. Finally, we have briefly considered the disproportionate detention of those from Black and Ethnic Minority groups and the implications this may have for nurses.

Activities: brief outline answers

Activity 8.1

- What warrant should have been sought?

James was already recalled, therefore section 135(2) is the appropriate warrant to enable the police to gain access to his property.

- Who could apply for it?

The police, an AMHP, a nurse from the hospital James is recalled to or a person authorised to do so by that organisation.

- What factors should be considered in planning James's admission?

The person coordinating the admission will need to do a risk assessment of the situation and seek to balance James's safety, as well as that of the professionals and the public, with James's dignity and not criminalising or stigmatising the admission. Their assessment should include James's view and they should seek to work in partnership with him as much as safe management of risk allows. It is important that each person involved knows their role and that James is supported to understand what is happening. Chapters 11.3 and 11.4 of the Code offer further factors to consider. Compare your list with what is in this guidance (Welsh Code Ch 9).

- Who can convey James?

The police, an AMHP, a nurse from the hospital James is recalled to or a person authorised to do so by that organisation.

Activity 8.2

The three parts are:

- the evidence of a mental disorder;
- the need for admission for assessment and/or treatment; and
- the risk to self or others.

If the person is admitted for treatment then there is also the further requirement that appropriate treatment is available and they are not detained purely for the purpose of confinement.

Activity 8.3

- What sections of the English and Welsh Code of Practice are relevant to this situation?

The English Code of Practice paragraphs 16.5 to 16.6; the Welsh Code of Practice 11.32.

- How are the guiding principles relevant?

The purpose of restricting access to the mobile phone and the risks to others must be considered alongside the least restrictive way of achieving the necessary outcome and how to involve the patient in the process.

- How could you limit the impact of any intervention?

You may want to consider other ways Martin can maintain contact with those important to him and how he can work with you towards getting his phone back.

- Who else may be able to assist the patient to understand the provisions around removing the mobile phone and advocate for them?

An IMHA or Martin's solicitor may be able to independently support him.

Further reading

Care Quality Commission and National Mental Health Development Unit (April 2011) Count me in 2010. **http://www.cqc.org.uk/sites/default/files/media/documents/count_me_in_2010_final_tagged.pdf**

Department of Health (2010) *Race Equality Action Plan: A five year review.* **www.nmhdu.org.uk/news/race-equality-action-plan-a-five-year-review**

Information on race equality.

Royal College of Psychiatrists (2008) *Standards on the Use of Section 136 of the MHA 1983.* London: Royal College of Psychiatrists.

Information on hospital places of safety.

Useful websites

http://www.blackmentalhealth.org.uk

http://www.mind.org.uk

http://www.rethink.org

Useful patient advocacy sites.

Multiple choice questions

1. What is the maximum time a person removed to a place of safety under section 135(1) can be kept there for?

   (a)   72 hours
   (b)   28 days
   (c)   Until the admitting nurse decides otherwise
   (d)   6 hours

2. Which of these sections enables a prisoner to be transferred from prison?

    (a)   Section 3
    (b)   Section 35
    (c)   Section 47
    (d)   Section 17

3. How often does a restricted hospital order have to be renewed?

    (a)   Every 6 months
    (b)   Every year
    (c)   Never
    (d)   After the first 28 days and then six monthly

4. With regard to detained patients subject to further restrictions, which of the following is correct?

    (a)   These are authorised by the detention and no further consideration needs to be given
    (b)   Restrictions should be based on individual risk assessments and not blanket bans
    (c)   Seclusion can only be used for forensic patients
    (d)   Only those who have committed serious offences are admitted to secure wards

Chapter 9
Best practice and the Mental Health Act: leadership and care

NMC Standards for Pre-registration Nursing Education

This chapter will address the following competencies:

Domain 1: Professional values

7. All nurses must be responsible and accountable for keeping their knowledge and skills up to date through continuing professional development. They must aim to improve their performance and enhance the safety and quality of care through evaluation, supervision and appraisal.
8. All nurses must practice independently, recognising the limits of their competence and knowledge. They must reflect on these limits and seek advice from, or refer to, other professionals where necessary.
9. All nurses must appreciate the value of evidence in practice, be able to understand and appraise research, apply relevant theory and research findings to their work, and identify areas for further investigation.

Domain 4: Leadership, management and team working

1. All nurses must act as change agents and provide leadership through quality improvement and service development to enhance people's wellbeing and experiences of healthcare.
2. All nurses must systematically evaluate care and ensure that they and others use the findings to help improve people's experience and care outcomes and to shape future services.

NMC Essential Skills Clusters

This chapter will address the following ESCs:

Cluster: Organisational aspects of care

11. People can trust the newly registered graduate nurse to safeguard children and adults from vulnerable situations and support and protect them from harm.

By the first progression point

1. Acts within legal frameworks and local policies in relation to safeguarding adults and children who are in vulnerable situations.

By entry to the register

9. Supports people in asserting their human rights

10. Challenges practices which do not safeguard those in need of support and protection.

14. People can trust the newly registered graduate nurse to be an autonomous and confident member of the multi-disciplinary or multi agency team and to inspire confidence in others.

By the second progression point

4. Reflects on own practice and discusses issues with other members of the team to enhance learning.

By entry to the register

9. Act as an effective role model in decision making, taking action and supporting others.

10. Works inter-professionally and autonomously as a means of achieving optimum outcomes for people.

Chapter aims

By the end of this chapter you will be able to:

- describe the ways in which nurses are legally accountable for their actions;
- understand the link between best practice and minimum standards of care;
- begin to apply this knowledge to practice under the Mental Health Act (MHA);
- name the four key offences defined within the MHA;
- reflect on the importance of safeguarding the rights and welfare of vulnerable adults already subject to compulsion and how this relates to safeguarding and whistle-blowing.

Introduction

The nursing profession is grounded in the strong values of care for patients and promoting their wellbeing. In fact these are often the reasons why many come into the profession. However, the profession and wider society continue to be shocked by investigations that highlight poor care and abuse of some of the most vulnerable groups. When working with detained patients you will be working with one of the most vulnerable groups: those deprived of their liberty. You will have a responsibility to ensure their care does not become abusive, for example withholding cigarette breaks from patients because they have absconded from the hospital or not complied with other parts of their care plan.

This chapter identifies the key ways nurses are accountable for their practice and how this relates to your carrying out care under the provisions of the MHA. It will stress the importance of your taking responsibility to ensure your practice is lawful and person-centred and enable you to identify appropriate steps to take if you observe poor practice. Throughout, you are reminded of the need to be mindful of the vulnerability of patients that are already subject to coercion and the need to ensure this does not turn into abuse.

The professional and legal responsibilities of nurses

Richard Griffith and Cassam Tengnah (2010) discuss the nurse's professional and legal obligations in detail in *Law and Professional Issues in Nursing*, which is part of the Learning Matters Transforming Nursing Practice Series. A key concept is *accountability*, which they define as *being answerable for your personal acts or omissions to a higher authority with whom you have a legal relationship* (p36) and describe it as performing two key functions: seeking to prevent harm and providing redress to those who are harmed. They go on to define four areas of law in which this accountability operates.

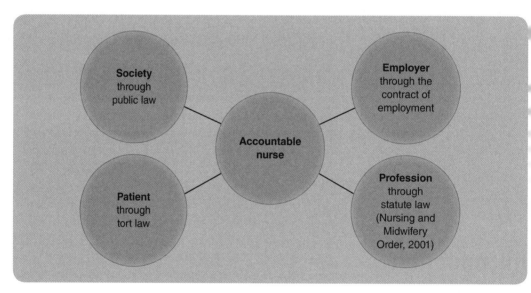

Figure 9.1: Four spheres of accountability.

Source: Griffith, R and Tengnah, C (2008) *Law and Professional Issues in Nursing.* Exeter: Learning Matters.

These include the general obligations that the law places on all of us. For example, the law requires everyone not to commit criminal offences. There are also the obligations specific to being a nurse. For example, your registration will be dependent on you upholding the Nursing and Midwifery Council (NMC) Code of Conduct and action can be taken against you if you are found to have failed this duty. In addition, they include obligations because you are employed by a specific organisation. For example, you have a duty to comply with the contract you have with your employer. This includes an obligation to carry out your duties with due care and diligence. A failure to do this could lead to disciplinary action.

Each of these areas of law has its own burden of proof and decision making procedures. These include the type of evidence that can be considered, the way investigations are carried out and the type of forum which considers the evidence and reaches decisions. Criminal offences have the most rigorous procedures and the highest burden of proof, whereas an employer taking disciplinary action need only *hold an honest and genuine belief that the employee is guilty of misconduct based on the outcome of a reasonable investigation* (p44). This can often lead to situations in which there is not sufficient evidence to prosecute a nurse for a criminal offence. However, an employer may still be able to take disciplinary proceedings against the nurse for not carrying out their duties with due care and diligence.

Concept summary: the Bolam test

The standard of care required in negligence cases is determined by the Bolam test, a court case from 1957. Mr Bolam was an informal mental health patient. He was receiving electro-convulsive therapy without the use of restraint or muscle relaxant. He flailed about in the procedure and suffered injuries. He claimed the injuries were caused by the hospital's negligence. As a part of their defence the hospital relied on the fact that it was common practice amongst doctors to use neither muscle relaxant, nor restraint and to only inform the patient of the risks if the patient requested.

As Griffith and Tengnah (2010) explain, in the context of nursing this means practice must not fall below that accepted by a respected body of professional opinion. Although this opinion or accepted practice does not need to be unanimous within the profession, it must be able to stand up to logical analysis. For example, a nurse could not rely on the fact that a practice was culturally accepted and common in their place of work as a justification for carrying out that practice themselves, if that practice was found to be poor. Furthermore, a registered nurse could not rely on inexperience as a defence against giving substandard care to her patients. What this shows is that you will be, as a registered professional, accountable for your own practice. As a result, it is also essential that you realise the limits of your own expertise and when you must involve others in order to ensure that patients always receive safe and effective care.

Scenario

As a newly registered nurse, you are carrying out one to one observations on Peter, who was admitted earlier that day under section 2 of the MHA with suspected depression and thoughts of self-harm. Your organisation has a set format to record these observations, which includes a risk assessment.

(continued)

continued ...

• *After a short while of being with Peter, he tells you that he has taken an overdose of a medication that*
• *you do not know. He tells you he doesn't know the exact number of tablets and is vague. You try,*
• *calmly, to get more information before reporting this to the nurse in charge. However, he tells you he*
• *doesn't want to talk about it anymore and that he had not really done this but just wanted you to*
• *know how unwell he was.*

Activity 9.1   *Decision making*

If your patient in the scenario had taken an overdose and needed physical treatment for it, could it be given under the MHA?

What should you do in this situation?

If Peter had taken an overdose and needed physical treatment for it, what would be the legal basis, or authority, for that treatment? You may find it helpful to reread Chapter 5.

There is an outline answer at the end of the chapter.

A note on best practice nursing on the ward today

This chapter so far has been concerned with preventing harm through ensuring accountability. This inevitably means defining a standard, such as the Bolam test, below which practice should not fall. However, as a registered nurse the NMC standards require you to go beyond a minimum level of care by taking responsibility to ensure your practice is continually developing and you are leading improvements in patient quality and safety. This will involve being aware of government guidance, findings of investigations and regulatory authorities and changes in case law, legislation and codes of practice. For example, this could include moving from an approach that sees those with mental disorder as the object of treatment to asking, in partnership with service users and others, what needs to be done to enable them to have greater control of their recovery and wider life choices, and how this can be balanced with ensuring their safety.

Achieving best practice can be challenging when faced with difficult decisions to which there is not always a choice that immediately appears right and there are significant consequences if things go wrong. Assessing a person before they go on leave may involve recognition that things could go wrong, but this is a justified risk because of the essential nature of the leave to their recovery. Whilst making a decision, it can often feel as though you will be damned if you do and damned if you don't. That is, you may fear that you will be criticised for applying unnecessary restrictions if you do not allow the leave but will also be criticised if you allow it and something goes wrong. However, another way of approaching the dilemma is to recognise that you will be undertaking tasks on behalf of a public body that involve key issues of liberty, welfare and the safety of others. It is therefore only right that when things go wrong, the decisions are scrutinised to determine any accountability and to enable learning. At the same time, you will be expected to justify a decision that restricts a person's autonomy because you are acting on behalf of the state and are required to give reasons for such actions. At the heart of this is accountability for decision making and learning.

As a registered nurse you will have an individual responsibility to demonstrate that you have appropriately made these types of decisions. This will inevitably mean fulfilling your professional duty to ensure that your practice remains up to date through ongoing training, research and practice development. Being aware of government guidance, findings of investigations and regulatory authorities, and changes to the Act or the Codes of Practice will also be important. As care and treatment for those detained under the Act evolves and changes, so too must your practice, in order to ensure you work within the parameters that would satisfy the Bolam test and the Code of Conduct. It will also mean being able to use the tools, policies and procedures of the organisation in which you work to support and demonstrate your decision making. However, it is important to recognise that being familiar with guidance and internal policies is essential to you fulfilling your individual nursing responsibility, but they do not take it away; you are the one who must be ultimately satisfied your practice is appropriate and safe. Perhaps this is demonstrated most clearly by the status of the Code of Practice. You have a duty to have regard to it but can depart from it providing you have cogent reasons to do so. In determining whether your reasons are cogent or not you will need to ask, amongst other things, if they comply with the wider requirements of the law and professional practice.

Scenario

You are working on a rehabilitation adult mental health ward. A patient, Jim, approaches you and asks if he can take his one and a half hour unescorted leave to the library, to research a college project. You remember that at handover a nurse expressed concerns that Jim had been isolating himself that morning. He has a history of significant self-harm when unwell.

Following staff expressing concern that they felt uncertain about making decisions around leave, the hospital introduced a standard process that involved considering the circumstances of leave (including its purpose and whether it was authorised), the current risk assessment concerning leave, the current mental state, the clothing and description of the person and the contingency plan if things go wrong. This was described as the 5Cs and all nurses were given guidance on how to follow the process and succinctly record their findings.

When you undertake this process, Jim admits his low mood and puts it down to concern about getting the research done. He says he does not have any thoughts or plans to self-harm. You note from the risk assessment that Jim can have low periods that he has been reliably able to self-report, has been seeking help when necessary and that achieving goals helps him. You agree that Jim will contact the ward on his mobile phone if his mood deteriorates or if he has any thoughts about self-harming. Finally, you record your assessment, reasoning and decision in the prescribed format.

Following such a process would support you in considering all the relevant information, diligently carrying out a balanced risk assessment and recording your findings and decision in a transparent way, whilst at the same time engaging with the patient to promote their recovery.

The MHA, Code of Practice and delegated duties

As should be clear from the previous chapters, the MHA places a number of duties on certain individuals and organisations and gives them various powers. Detaining organisations can then delegate to appropriate members of staff through a scheme of delegation that is agreed by the board of the organisation. Nurses could be delegated a number of tasks including receiving detention papers, informing a patient of their rights, escorting a patient on leave, taking into custody and returning an absent without leave (AWOL) patient, actions in connection with managing challenging behaviour, managing authorised leave on a day to day basis and authorising transfers of patients to hospitals run by other organisations.

As with all care that you provide to any patient, the above activities will require you to draw upon your key nursing skills, many of which we have highlighted in the introduction to each chapter of this book. However, they will also include activities on which the Code of Practice gives specific guidance. For example, there are chapters giving guidance on explaining to patients their rights and managing challenging behaviour. As explained in Chapter 1 and above, nurses are one of the professional groups that has a duty to have regard for the Code of Practice when carrying out tasks for which it gives guidance. Although local policies and practices should be reviewed in accordance with this guidance, you have your own responsibility as a nurse to keep up to date on it.

Acts done without 'bad faith or without reasonable care'

As you will appreciate by now, the MHA is a powerful and complex piece of legislation. It is powerful because it gives some people in society rights to restrict the liberties of others and to give treatment or carry out certain procedures on others which would, in other circumstances, be illegal. It is a complex piece of legislation because within those broad headings there are many other subdivisions, each designed to provide checks and balances. For you, this means that, if it were not for the Act being in place, you would have no defence in law to carry out certain activities and you would therefore be in breach, possibly of other laws and of your professional nursing standards. On the other hand, if you failed to undertake certain of these duties or activities when they did come within the scope of the MHA, you could be committing the same faults.

Activity 9.2 *Reflection*

Make a list of some of the acts that you consider the MHA gives you a power or a duty to undertake, that would otherwise be in breach of your professional nursing standards or be unlawful. You may find it helpful to refer to earlier chapters as you carry out this activity. Before you continue, check your answers with those given at the end of the book.

Keep these in mind as you read on about how the law seeks to both protect you whilst undertaking these acts and ensure that those detained are not subject to abuse.

There is an outline answer at the end of the chapter.

The MHA acknowledges that, as set out in the purpose principle, the reason acts are undertaken under its provisions is to promote the recovery and safety of patients and others. It does this by providing a high level of protection to those carrying out the acts. In fact any civil or criminal proceedings, in relation to acts purporting to have been done in pursuance of the MHA, can only be taken out if permission is given by the High Court (civil) or by the Director of Public Prosecutions (criminal) and that it is shown the act was done in bad faith or without reasonable care. This includes three of the offences described in the next section but does not include the offence of ill-treatment or wilful neglect. Although certain organisations are exempt from this protection, it does include nurses. However, it is worth noting that this protection has been subject to certain human rights challenges. For example, in *TTM* v. *LB Hackney* [2011] EWCA Civ 4 this protection was not given to the actions of an approved mental health professional (AMHP) which were argued to have made a detention unlawful and to which the local authority were vicariously liable. It is therefore important that in your practice, you recognise the vulnerability of those already subject to coercive powers and ensure you have authority to undertake any actions. If you are concerned that the authority of any actions being asked of you is not sound then it is advisable to seek clarification or advice from the leads in your organisation, preferably before any incident.

Section summary

This section has explored the legal responsibilities of a nurse and the varying ways in which they are held accountable for their practice. We have explored this in the context of practice under the MHA. In particular, we have explored the ways in which you are accountable, and have looked at practical steps you can take to develop a transparent and defensible practice. Finally, we have briefly explored how the MHA seeks to balance the rights of those subject to its powers with the need for staff to be able to confidently undertake their duties.

Offences under the MHA

Apart from actions sanctioned by the MHA, that would otherwise be an offence, those detained under the MHA have the same protection from wider laws that we all enjoy. Furthermore, the MHA offers further protection to patients who come under it by establishing a number of offences. These will be relevant to you as a nurse, both in relation to yourself, the practice of others and the actions of third parties. The offences are set out in section 126 to section 130. There are four offences.

First, it is an offence to forge or make false statements in applications or recommendations for detention or other documents made under the Act. This can include the omission of key details. The Act also contains conflict of interest regulations in relation to those assessing for detention, the purpose of which is to ensure assessments are objective. Although it may seem unlikely that the powers of the Act will, today, be used to detain people for nefarious reasons, it is right that there is a deterrent in place to prevent this and that justice can be done if the Act is used in this way. This offence also helps to ensure the procedures of the Act are properly followed. For example, say in the course of your duties you identify an error to mental health paperwork that undermines its authority, perhaps an AMHP not signing an application that has already been accepted and used as authority to detain. The AMHP would potentially be committing an offence if they were then asked to sign it and did, particularly if it was made to appear that the paperwork was signed when it was initially accepted. In these circumstances the correct course of action for you to take would be to inform those responsible for scrutinising the papers of your concern that there is an error that undermines the authority to detain. It is normally mental health administrators who perform this role. They will then be responsible for taking steps to remedy the situation. This could include a further assessment under the MHA.

Second, it is an offence for a staff member of a hospital, including managers, to ill-treat or wilfully neglect an inpatient receiving treatment for mental disorder or to ill-treat or wilfully neglect, on the premises of a hospital or care home, an outpatient receiving treatment for mental disorder. Under this section, it is also an offence for a person to ill-treat or wilfully neglect a person who is subject to their guardianship or in their custody or care. This offence can lead to a prison sentence of up to five years.

Third, it as an offence to assist or induce a detained patient to abscond from a hospital, or a person subject to guardianship, community treatment order (CTO) or detention to absent themselves from a place where they are required to be; likewise, to harbour or prevent, hinder or interfere with attempts to take them into custody. The offence can lead to a prison sentence of up to two years.

Finally, it is an offence to obstruct, without reasonable cause, certain acts from being undertaken if those acts are undertaken in the course of a person's duty under the Act. These include the inspection of any premises and the interviewing, visiting or examination of a person by a person authorised to do so. This offence also includes the failure to produce any document required for inspection by an authorised person. The offence can lead to a prison sentence of up to three months. Possible examples of this offence are refusing to allow an AMHP to interview a person under the Act or refusing to allow a Care Quality Commission (CQC) inspector carrying out an inspection under this Act from undertaking that inspection.

A local social services authority can institute proceedings under this Act for all the offences. However, in the case of ill-treatment and neglect they need the approval of the Director of Public Prosecutions.

Case study

BBC TV's Panorama *carried out an investigation into Winterbourne View, a specialist hospital for people with learning disabilities. Their investigation followed concerns expressed to them by a whistle-blower and revealed evidence of what a judge later described as a 'culture of cruelty'. The documentary televised on the BBC included recordings, taken secretly, of residents being slapped,*

> *soaked in water, sworn at, trapped under chairs and having their hair pulled and eyes poked by some staff members. Following a police investigation, 11 care workers, comprising two nurses and nine support workers, were convicted of the offence of ill-treatment or wilful neglect, as defined by the MHA. One offender was sentenced to two years in prison.*

The above incident is a powerful example and reminder of why explicit protection for this vulnerable group is still needed, particularly for those who are cared for in institutions where they have limited contact with the outside world and where those outside the institution have limited access. The abusive care that occurred was not just caused by individual actions but is an example of situations in which safeguards fail to prevent a culture that accepts such abuse as normal. The abuse was only brought to light following the brave actions of a whistle-blower.

> ### Section summary
>
> This section has reviewed the offences that are defined in the MHA to protect the rights of vulnerable groups with mental disorder and hold others to account when those rights are transgressed.

Safeguarding

When working with patients under the MHA, you may work both with children and vulnerable adults. These individuals are likely to be at a greater risk of abuse for a variety of reasons, including that their rights and autonomy are already being restricted and controlled by staff, the ward environment itself, by fact of their mental health or due to complex social situations in which they may have been living. As we discussed, by virtue of this they may need to be protected from abuse from staff, other patients or members of the public. It may also be that the patients themselves pose a risk to others that the organisation has a duty to address. It will, therefore, be important that you are familiar with the safeguarding policies of your employer for both children and adults.

The legislation and guidance for safeguarding is clear that safeguarding is everyone's duty. This is also clear in the standards of pre-registration nursing at the start of the chapter. The example of Winterbourne View is another patent example of how care that involves coercion will be abusive if it is not undertaken with the appropriate values, with proper authority and in a manner consistent with the relevant safeguards. You have a responsibility not only to ensure your practice meets these standards but also to be mindful of others' practice and to address this appropriately when it does not. A nurse's commitment to individual responsibility and strong leadership is key to preventing institutional abuse, as was seen at Winterbourne View.

Concept summary

Institutional abuse is an important concept in *No Secrets: Guidance on developing and implementing multi-agency policies and procedures to protect vulnerable adults from abuse* (Department of Health, 2000). In the context of abuse against vulnerable adults, it comments:

> *Neglect and poor professional practice also need to be taken into account. This may take the form of isolated incidents of poor or unsatisfactory professional practice, at one end of the spectrum, through to pervasive ill treatment or gross misconduct at the other. Repeated instances of poor care may be an indication of more serious problems and this is sometimes referred to as institutional abuse.*
> (p10)

Scenario

You are working on a psychiatric intensive care unit (PICU) where Kelly has been detained for five months, initially on section 2 and now on section 3. Kelly has recently had her medication changed. She had capacity to consent to this treatment and did so. The responsible clinician (RC) completed a T2. Recently Kelly has been reluctant to take the medication due to the side effects it has on her sexual drive. You are present during an incident when a nurse is asking her to take her medication. You hear the nurse tell Kelly that she is detained so, if she continues to refuse it, she will end up being prescribed a depot injection and restrained if necessary.

Activity 9.3	*Leadership and management*

Consider this scenario and answer the following questions.

- Is this potentially a safeguarding issue?
- How is this a misrepresentation of the powers of the MHA?
- What steps could be taken to enable the patient to exercise these rights?
- What steps would you take in regard to your colleague?

There is an outline answer at the end of the chapter.

It may also be that in carrying out safeguarding duties you are acting under powers set out in the MHA. This is likely to involve some of the powers that are more specifically addressed in the Code of Practice. These include searching, restricting visiting, restricting access to mobile phones, observations and the management of challenging behaviour. For example, treatment under the

MHA includes the management of risk associated with the manifestation of a person's mental illness, for which they are detained and this can include, amongst other things, observation and restricting movement. The proper exercise of these powers can lead to the person and others being effectively safeguarded.

Case study

Jane is detained on a PICU ward. She has a diagnosis of bipolar disorder, is in a manic phase and is sexually disinhibited. In the past, when in a manic phase, she has been vulnerable to sexual advances from others which she would normally refuse. The memories of these continue to be traumatic to her. There are others on the ward that may also be vulnerable to disinhibited behaviour. Both they and Jane are vulnerable adults and there is a duty on the hospital to safeguard them. At the same time, the MHA gives powers to hospital staff to take specific actions to manage risk associated with the mental disorder. In this case, they include suspending Jane's leave, increasing observations to one to one and reviewing and changing her medication. Using these powers also enables the hospital staff to meet their duty to safeguard Jane and the other vulnerable adults, whilst ensuring any restrictions on Jane are proportionate and necessary.

Section summary

This section has briefly explored the link between safeguarding and the MHA. The importance of upholding the rights and safeguards of those who already have their autonomy restricted and who are subject to lawful coercion has been emphasised. In addition we have briefly looked at how the powers of the MHA can be appropriately used as part of a safeguarding plan.

Whistle-blowing

Whistle-blowing is generally defined as an employee raising an issue about danger or unlawfulness that affects others. This can be (an issue) within their own organisation or an outside organisation.

The law does offer protection to whistle-blowers in certain situations and if certain criteria are met. First of all, the concern must be one that the Employment Rights Act 1996 defines as a protected disclosure. That is, it must be that: a criminal offence has been, is about to be, or is likely to be committed; a person has failed or is about to fail to comply with a legal obligation imposed upon them (this includes an obligation imposed upon them by a contract of employment); the health and safety of any person has been, is being, or is likely to be endangered; a miscarriage of justice has occurred, is occurring, or is likely to occur; the environment has been, is being, or is likely to be damaged; or information tends to show that one of the above matters has been or is likely to be deliberately concealed.

The employee need only have a reasonable belief that the event has occurred or will do so. If this disclosure is made within the employing organisation in good faith, the worker is protected from detriment. This is the preferred route of disclosure, as it enables the relevant person in the employing organisation to address the issue and is likely to be the most expedient.

However, as is evident from the example of Winterbourne View, there are situations in which the normal safeguards do not protect vulnerable groups from abuse. In this situation, before approaching the BBC the whistle-blower had attempted to raise the issues with the organisation and with the CQC, but with no satisfaction. The law does offer whistle-blowers protection in these circumstances but there are further criteria that have to be met.

If the disclosure is made to a legal advisor or is in line with a policy of the employing organisation, then it is protected. It is also protected if it is made to a person prescribed by the Public Interest Disclosure (Prescribed Persons) Order 1999/1549.

Situation	Prescribed person
Provision of healthcare	CQC
Provision of healthcare by and for Welsh National Health Service (NHS) bodies	Healthcare Inspectorate Wales
Issues concerning the regulation and performance of NHS foundation trusts	Independent Regulator of NHS Foundation Trusts

Table 9.1: Public Interest Disclosure (Prescribed Persons) Order 1999/1549.

If the disclosure is made to other persons then further requirements must be met. The employee must not have acted for personal gain. Additionally, they must have reasonably believed that their employer would have subjected them to detriment if a disclosure was made internally, or that the evidence relating to the alleged failure would either be concealed or destroyed, or that an internal disclosure had already been made. Finally the employee must show that the disclosure was reasonable in all the circumstances of the case. Whether these requirements are met can be a complicated issue, even for solicitors.

Case study

Following concerns regarding serious failings at Mid Staffordshire NHS Foundation Trust, Robert Francis QC was asked to chair an independent inquiry. This culminated in February 2013 in what is known as the 'Francis Report' and more formally as the 'Report of the Mid Staffordshire NHS Foundation Trust Public Inquiry' (see Useful websites). The inquiry found significant evidence of patients being placed at serious risk due to inadequate care. It found that the organisation failed to listen to its staff and patients and failed *to challenge an insidious negative culture involving a tolerance of poor standards and a disengagement from managerial and leadership responsibilities. In his covering letter to the Secretary of State for Health, Robert Francis set out the aims of his recommendations. These concerned the establishment of agreed standards of care, processes and systems to enable them to happen and be monitored, and a culture that facilitates positive care. In particular they included:* Foster a common culture shared by all in the service of putting the patient first, Ensure openness, transparency and candour throughout the system about matters of concern and Make all those who provide care for patients – individuals and organisations – properly accountable for what they do and to ensure that the public is protected from those not fit to provide such a service.

The ability to inform third parties to bring abuse to light is a necessary avenue. However, it cannot replace the need for NHS organisations to develop a learning culture that is transparent, listens to those who raise concerns and seeks to identify appropriate accountability. Indeed, all third parties can do is highlight the issues; these can only be addressed if the organisation delivering the care addresses them or another organisation takes over. As a newly qualified nurse, you will be bringing a fresh eye to bear on culturally accepted practices and will be in a unique position to raise any concerns or promote best practice. This can be daunting, as the fear is that you may not be taken seriously or be penalised. However, learning how to raise issues appropriately with colleagues, managers and within the wider organisation, and how your organisation seeks to address these, can be your first steps in developing strong leadership.

Section summary

This section has explored the protection the law provides to nurses and others when they raise concerns about patient safety or care. It has set out the different circumstances in which this protection allows concerns to be raised internally and externally. Finally, it has highlighted the need for organisations to be able to take responsibility and learn from mistakes and how a newly qualified nurse can begin to develop these skills.

Chapter summary

In this chapter you have been introduced to the way the law ensures nurses are accountable for their practice and the relationship this has to other safeguards that are aimed at preventing poor or abusive care. You will have begun to understand the importance of ensuring your practice is kept up to date, your duties are carried out with due care and diligence and how your practice can be both defensible and person-centred. You will be able to recognise how the policies and procedures of your organisation can support you in this and when you may have a duty to have regard to the guidance in the MHA Code of Practice. Finally, you should be able to understand the vulnerability to abuse of groups already subject to coercive powers and how developing your leadership skills can be a safeguard against this.

Activities: brief outline answers

Activity 9.1

1. Treatment for which the purpose is to treat the outcome of self-harm related to the person's mental disorder is likely to be treatment that comes under section 63 of the MHA, and can be given under the direction of an approved clinician (AC) without the consent of the patient. However, before directing any treatment the AC will need to make a balanced judgement considering, amongst other things, the risks, views of the patient, any coercion that may be needed and the least restrictive options.
2. As you are unaware of the risks associated with the possible overdose and the signs associated with it, you should seek more expert advice. Your observations and recordings will be an important part of the evidence used to make a decision. You should record your decision making and communicate this to the patient in an appropriate way.

Activity 9.2

Examples could include administering medication without consent, forcing a person to return to the ward, transferring a patient without consent and restraining a person who is trying to leave the ward. In some circumstances authority from these acts could come from the Mental Capacity Act or common law.

Activity 9.3

1. This is potentially a safeguarding issue. The powers of coercion under the MHA are not being properly explained to the patient. The hospital has a duty under section 132 to ensure the patient understands their rights. This could be due to a lack of understanding by the individual nurse, a culture on the ward that misunderstands the legal powers of the MHA, or deliberate misrepresentation.
2. Although the patient had consented to this treatment, they are entitled to withdraw that consent at any time. The patient's reasons for this may lead to a change in the treatment plan that they then consent to. If, after ruling out less restrictive alternatives, the RC is still of a view that the treatment with medication of a mental disorder needs to proceed and that the legal tests to allow this were met, they would need a second opinion appointed doctor (SOAD) to approve the treatment before it could proceed. The SOAD is not a rubber stamping exercise and they may not approve the treatment or they may require it to be adjusted. If the SOAD does authorise treatment, they have a duty to give reasons for their decision which the RC must communicate to the patient, unless there are clinical reasons that would justify not doing so.
3. The RC and/or the lead nurse should ensure the patient understands their rights under the MHA and the safeguards around their treatment. The support of an independent mental health advocate (IMHA) around these issues could also be facilitated. Finally, the patient should be aware of their right to complain to the CQC and, if they have been administered medication when there was not lawful authority to do so, then they should be advised of how to seek legal advice should they wish.
4. What steps you should take would depend on the nature of your concern and the policies of your employing organisation. If the nurse concerned misunderstands the powers of the MHA, it may be that, in the first instance, you can discuss this with your colleague and raise any possible need for training within your team and with your manager. It may be that this leads to process change in relation to the administering of medication under the MHA and the reissuing or writing of guidance for the nursing staff.

Further reading

Bach, S and Ellis P (2011) *Leadership, Management and Team Working in Nursing.* Exeter: Learning Matters.

Information on leadership and nursing.

Griffith, R and Tengnah, C (2010) *Law and Professional Issues in Nursing.* Exeter: Learning Matters.

Information on the professional and legal responsibilities and accountabilities of nurses.

Useful websites

https://www.gov.uk/government/publications/safeguarding-adults-the-role-of-health-services

Up to date Department of Health guidance on safeguarding adults.

https://www.gov.uk/whistleblowing/overview

Information regarding protection for whistle-blowers.

http://www.midstaffspublicinquiry.com/report

The Francis Report.

Multiple choice questions

1. Which of the following are areas of law that ensure nurses are accountable when practising under the Mental Health Act?

    (a)   Public law, tort law, contract of employment, statute
    (b)   Asking 'Would I want my family cared for in my place of work?'
    (c)   Only criminal law
    (d)   Providing I follow the Mental Health Act, other areas of law don't apply

2. What protection does the Mental Health Act provide for those carrying out acts in pursuance of it?

    (a)   They are protected from liability unless the act was done in bad faith or without reasonable care
    (b)   No more protection than any other act a nurse undertakes
    (c)   Complete protection from liability
    (d)   Protection providing their act is not criminal

3. The misrepresentation of the powers of the Mental Health Act is:

    (a)   Not significant providing the patient's best interest is at heart
    (b)   Potentially a safeguarding issue
    (c)   Always a criminal offence
    (d)   Always a case of deliberate deception

4. Which of the following is necessary in order for a whistle-blower to have protection when informing a party that is not their employer, a legal adviser or a prescribed person?

    (a)   The disclosure must not have been made for personal gain
    (b)   The act must be a criminal offence
    (c)   The person must have informed their employer first
    (d)   They must be certain the act has occurred

Chapter 10
Tribunals and managers' hearings

9. Provides accurate and comprehensive written and verbal reports based on best available evidence.

14. People can trust the newly registered graduate nurse to be an autonomous and confident member of the multi-disciplinary or multi agency team and to inspire confidence in others.

Entry to the register

6. Actively consults and explores solutions and ideas with others to enhance care.

10. Works inter-professionally and autonomously as a means of achieving optimum outcomes for people.

Chapter aims

By the end of this chapter you will be able to:

- understand the key differences between managers' hearings and tribunals;
- know the panel members that make up each;
- understand the key powers each has;
- know your duties in terms of submitting oral and written evidence;
- understand how patients experience tribunals and managers' hearings;
- begin to reflect on how you can intervene to ensure patients receive a more positive experience.

Introduction

The right to have a court consider the grounds for a person's detention is a key human right. However, these forums can often seem confusing and impenetrable to patients, making it difficult for them to exercise these rights in a meaningful way.

This chapter will explore two forums through which a patient can challenge their detention: tribunals and managers' hearings. It will enable you to understand the make-up of each panel, their powers and the procedures they follow. The chapter will focus on what will be expected of you at the hearings and how you can use your knowledge to improve patients' experiences.

Statutory footing of tribunals and managers' hearings

Managers' hearings and tribunals are the two means by which patients can appeal against their detention or community treatment order (CTO) and by which these are automatically reviewed. Although there are similarities between them, there are more significant differences.

First Tier Tribunal (Mental Health)

The Tribunals Courts and Enforcement Act 2007 changed the structure of tribunals, establishing a single tribunal service and creating a First Tier Tribunal and an Upper Tribunal. Within these there are chambers dealing with different areas of practice. Mental health tribunals come under the 'Health, Education and Social Care Chamber'.

Concept summary: First Tier Tribunal (Mental Health)

The First Tier Tribunals (Mental Health) hear applications or references of patients liable to be detained under the Mental Health Act (MHA) or subject to CTOs and are governed by the Tribunal Procedure (First-tier Tribunal) (Health, Education and Social Care Chamber) Rules 2008 (TPR). They have many powers in common with courts but have the advantage of having experts in the field on their panel and being able to be less formal to help engage the patient. Their overriding objective is to ensure cases are heard justly and fairly. This includes:

(a) dealing with the case in ways which are proportionate to the importance of the case, the complexity of the issues, the anticipated costs and the resources of the parties;
(b) avoiding unnecessary formality and seeking flexibility in the proceedings;
(c) ensuring, so far as practicable, that the parties are able to participate fully in the proceedings;
(d) using any special expertise of the tribunal effectively; and
(e) avoiding delay, so far as compatible with proper consideration of the issues.

Decisions of the First Tier Tribunal can be appealed on points of law. Depending on the situation the appeal may be dealt with by the Upper Tribunal or the First Tier Tribunal.

The key difference between the First Tier Tribunal and the Upper Tribunal is that the former hears initial cases but the Upper Tribunal only hears appeals of those cases. In doing so, the Upper Tribunal can set precedent, which First Tier Tribunals must follow.

The Tribunal Service is completely independent of the organisation that manages the hospital. It also meets the requirements of the European Convention of Human Rights to have one's detention reviewed speedily by a court. As such, it is a significant safeguard in ensuring that patients are only detained when the legal criteria in the Act are met. In the 2011/12 financial year the Tribunal office held 16,048 hearings, had 4,431 applications withdrawn and in 7,559 cases applications were made but the responsible clinician (RC) discharged the patient before a hearing. Figure 10.1 gives details of the outcome of those hearings. Of those cases, 2,512 involved restricted patients. Figure 10.2 highlights that in almost 25 per cent of cases there was some form of discharge.

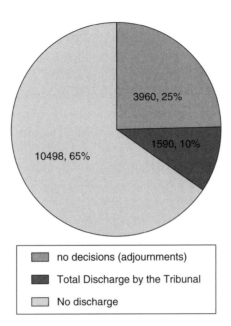

Figure 10.1: First Tier Tribunals' outcomes, 2011/12.

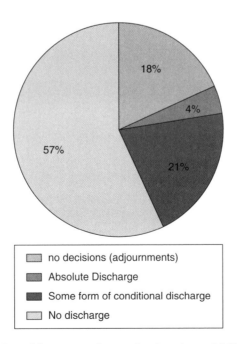

Figure 10.2: First Tier Tribunals' outcomes for restricted patients, 2011/12.

Source: Care Quality Commission Mental Health Act Annual Report 2011/12.

In addition to these formal outcomes, the hearings may also have led to positive outcomes for the patient following recommendations by the tribunal or scrutiny of the patient's case. It may also have enabled the patient to better understand any reasons for detention.

The rules governing exactly when a patient can apply to a tribunal can be complex and are beyond the scope of this book. The *Reference Guide to the Mental Health Act 1983* (Department of Health, 2008a) sets the rules out in detail and should be consulted when nurses are keeping individual patients informed of their rights. As a general rule of thumb, unrestricted patients have the right to apply to a tribunal once in every period of detention or CTO. For section 2 patients this must be within the first 14 days of the detention. For unrestricted patients detained under Part III, their first right to a tribunal is in their first period of renewal. For restricted patients, their rights to apply are once in every year but not in the first six months or first six months following a recall to hospital. Finally, nearest relatives have certain rights to apply to a tribunal for unrestricted patients to be discharged. This includes following an RC blocking a nearest relative's use of their power of discharge and following them being displaced as a nearest relative by a county court.

It is important that nurses keep patients correctly informed of their rights to apply, particularly section 2 patients, as a failure to do so may mean the patient is not enabled to exercise their right to a review by a court.

In addition to a patient's rights to appeal to a tribunal, the detaining organisation and the Secretary of State have duties to refer certain cases to the tribunal. These are set out in Chapter 23 of the *Reference Guide* and organisations will generally have systems in place to monitor this and refer appropriate cases. These rules can be complex and nurses would be advised to seek guidance in individual cases.

Managers' hearings

Concept summary: 'associate hospital manager'

Associate hospital manager is often the term used to describe a panel member of a 'manager's hearing'. They are not allowed to be employees of the organisation and so are usually volunteers or non-executive directors. Non-executive directors are board members of National Health Service (NHS) organisations that are not employed by that organisation. In organisations that are not foundation trusts, an associate hospital manager must be a member of the board or a committee or subcommittee authorised for the purpose. The Code of Practice states that organisations must ensure they are competent in the role and the working of the Act and receive training to understand the law, work with patients and professionals, reach sound judgements and properly record decisions. However, as they are lay people, they will rely more heavily on the evidence provided by professionals.

Managers' hearings are made up of panels of associate hospital managers. The hearings are in effect a way of the organisation reviewing the detention or CTO of any of its patients and ensuring the criteria are met.

The only rules and guidance regarding managers' hearings are in section 23 of the Mental Health Act and Chapter 31 of the Code of Practice. They have none of the court-like powers of tribunals. Patients can apply to have their detention reviewed as many times as they wish but the organisation does not have to automatically hold a formal review each time. In addition the organisation must arrange for a review each time a Part II patient's CTO or detention is renewed.

There is no national collation of the outcomes of these hearings.

Now we have explored the statutory footing of tribunals and managers' hearings, how patients can apply for each, and when automatic hearings occur, we will go on to look at the constitution of each.

The members of a tribunal and of a managers' hearing panel

Tribunals

The tribunal is made up of a judge and two members. One of the members has to be a medical member, who is a consultant psychiatrist. The judge and the medical member have specialist roles on the panel. The judge is responsible for chairing the panel and ensuring the requirements of law are met, taking a lead in drafting the reasons for a decision and signing the record of the tribunal.

The medical member has two roles. They are a decision making member of the panel but they also have a duty to interview the patient, review their records and form an opinion of the patient's medical condition. In order to prevent unfairness, the medical member should explain their roles to the patient. Otherwise, the patient may not realise the views formed at the interview will be used to inform the decision of the panel and may mistakenly believe the interview is confidential. The medical member should also share with all the parties of the tribunal any differing views they have from other medical witnesses. A failure to do this would lead to a situation in which the tribunal were making decisions on information others did not have a chance to challenge.

The third member is formally known as the tribunal member, but often referred to as the lay member. They usually have significant experience in a relevant health and social care field and can provide balance to ensure the proceedings are not dominated by a medical view.

Research summary

In March 2011 the Care Quality Commission (CQC) and the Administrative Justice and Tribunals Council published their results of jointly commissioned research, *Patients' Experiences of the First-tier Tribunal (Mental Health)*. Within the research, patients were asked about their experience of the medical member's interview. The responses included a very mixed view of their experience and the type of questions they were asked. A quarter of patients reported that the medical member did not explain that the results of the interview would be shared with the panel. The research recommended further training for medical members and that staff of the hospital take on a role in explaining the role of the medical member.

Enabling patients to understand the role of the medical member is key to ensuring that you facilitate equalities of power in relationships.

Hospital managers' panels

If the hospital arranges for the detention to be reviewed by a hearing, then three or more associate hospital managers must consider the case.

Section summary

In this section we have explored the roles of the panel members of tribunals and managers' hearings. We have highlighted the expert nature of the tribunal panel compared to the lay members that make up the panel for managers' hearings. We have also considered the implications for patients' understanding of the process, and of how each will consider your evidence.

The powers of tribunals and managers' hearings

Tribunals

As discussed earlier a tribunal is the way a patient can have a speedy review of their detention. A tribunal's powers are essential in ensuring this occurs. First Tier Tribunals have powers both in relation to controlling the proceedings themselves and in relation to the statutory regime to which the patient is subject. The powers in relation to the proceedings include case management powers that are mainly used before the tribunal itself meets but can also be used after the tribunal has begun. In practice, this means giving directions for the submission of reports, attendance and when hearings are to occur. These powers ensure that the tribunal is provided with sufficient evidence to hear the case fairly and that the necessary parties attend. Delays in tribunals due to late or insufficient reports can lead to a person's rights to a speedy review of their detention being denied. In recent years tribunals have sought to prevent this by being more proactive with the timescales within which reports must be submitted. Failure to comply with directions could lead to the matter being referred to the Upper Tribunal, who can impose financial penalties.

Other powers in relation to the proceedings include the power to exclude or include people from the tribunal. The power to include people is often used to allow observers. Before presenting evidence at your first tribunal, it may be that you have the opportunity to observe one. Before deciding whether to allow this, the judge has to consider guidance given by the Chamber President (*Guidance for the Observation of Tribunal Hearings,* **http://www.justice.gov.uk/downloads/ tribunals/mental-health/publications/GuidanceForObservationOfTribunal.pdf**), and must consider the impact on and respect the views of the patient and their representative. The tribunal should also ensure that you are aware of your duty to not make information public. It would be good practice for this to have been explored with the patient and their representative before the judge is approached.

Finally, the tribunal also has powers to decide if the hearing should be in private or public and to withhold information from the patient. The latter of these powers will be discussed below.

Case study: *AH v. West London MHT* [2011] UKUT 74 (AAC) (17 February 2011)

AH was a long term patient at Broadmoor high security hospital, detained under section 37/41. In total he had been detained for approximately 23 years. He had also had a recent change in diagnosis. He appealed to the Upper Tribunal, wishing for his case to be held in private. In considering the case, the Upper Tribunal made reference to the Convention on the Rights of Persons with Disabilities (CPRD). This is an international treaty which the UK has ratified and which seeks the full and equal enjoyment of human rights for those with disabilities. The Upper Tribunal granted his right to such a hearing. In doing so, they stated that such cases should ask: (a) Is it consistent with the subjective and informed wishes of the applicant (assuming he is competent to make an informed choice)? (b) Will it have an adverse effect on his mental health in the short or long term, taking account of the views of those treating him and any other expert views? (c) Are there any other special factors for or against a public hearing? (d) Can practical arrangements be made for an open hearing without disproportionate burden on the authority?

A key purpose of the powers in relation to the proceedings is to ensure that the patient receives a fair review of their detention or the statutory regime to which they are subject. At the start of the chapter we emphasised how difficult it can be for anyone to navigate these forums. In addition as detained patients are a particularly vulnerable group, there is a higher importance of them having a legal representative in order to ensure that they can effectively do this and exercise their rights. This is recognised in the fact that legal representation is available and that a tribunal can appoint a legal representative for a patient, in the event of the patient stating that they do not want to represent themselves, they wish to be represented or in the event the patient lacks capacity to appoint a representative. A representative has a right to be given the documents connected to the proceedings and meet with the patient.

With regard to the regime itself, the key powers of the tribunal are set out in Table 10.1.

The tribunal may also hear cases of patients transferred from prison and subject to restrictions or limited directions. It has more limited powers in these cases. For more information, see pages 193 and 194 of the *Reference Guide to the Mental Health Act 1983* (Department of Health, 2008a). Finally, the Secretary of State for Justice may authorise the removal from the UK of certain detained patients who do not have the right to live in the UK, but only if they have obtained the approval of a tribunal.

As well as the more formal powers, the tribunal can benefit patients in a number of ways. For example, they will often make non-statutory recommendations in regard to restricted patients to

	In relation to discharge	In relation to recommendations
Unrestricted detained patients	Must discharge the patient if it is not satisfied the criteria are met. May also discharge the patient under a discretionary power to discharge. May also order discharge at a future point.	May recommend leave, transfer or the making of a CTO and may consider the case further if the recommendation is not complied with.
Restricted detained patients	Must discharge the patient absolutely if it is not satisfied the criteria are met *and* it is satisfied that *it is not appropriate for the patient to remain liable to be recalled to hospital for further treatment.* Must discharge the patient conditionally if it is not satisfied the criteria for detention are met; *and* are not satisfied that *it is not appropriate for the patient to remain liable to be recalled to hospital for further treatment* (Department of Health, 2008a). May defer a conditional discharge whilst arrangements necessary for the discharge are made to its satisfaction.	
Conditionally discharged patients	Vary any conditions, impose new conditions or end the restriction order.	
CTO patients	Must discharge the patient if it is not satisfied the criteria are met.	
Guardianship patients	Must discharge the patient if the criteria for discharge are met. May also discharge the patient under a discretionary power to discharge.	

Table 10.1: Powers of the tribunal.

support an RC's application to the Ministry of Justice for leave or transfer. Perhaps one of the key advantages is that, through and in anticipation of questioning and encouraging, they focus minds, scrutinise decisions and evidence, clarify plans for discharge and identify positives.

Managers' hearings

The only formal power managers' panels have is to discharge patients from the statutory regime to which they are subject. In the case of restricted patients, they need the agreement of the Secretary of State. The panel may only discharge the patient if a majority agree, which consists of at least three people. In deciding this they apply the detention criteria but also have a discretionary power of discharge. In the case of a hearing occurring following an RC using their power to block a nearest relative's power of discharge, the panel also applies the criteria of 'dangerousness' but has a residual power not to discharge if this specific criteria is not met.

Some hospitals permit associate hospital managers to make informal recommendations. These could be about the specific case or about wider issues that have been identified in the process of the hearing. Similarly to tribunals, it is these informal powers that can often be of most benefit to the patient.

Scenario

James had been detained under section 3 at a rehabilitation unit. At a manager's hearing he was able to listen to and question the reasons for the restrictions on him. He was also able to talk about the importance of visiting his parents and the frustrations of only being able to spend a small amount of time with them, due to the restrictions on his leave and the distance at which they live. It became clear that this was affecting his attitudes towards his wider care plans and his recovery. Although James was not discharged, the panel recommended that the care team give greater consideration to enabling James to spend more time with his parents and explore what resources are available to enable this.

Although such a recommendation is not binding, as a nurse you have a duty to advocate appropriately for the patient and pursue person-centred care planning. The recommendations could both support and direct you in pursuing these ends.

Section summary

This section has explored the formal and informal powers of tribunals and managers' hearings. It has referred to the more extensive case management powers of tribunals and has highlighted the need to ensure that you complete accurate and up to date reports and submit them on time. The different powers of each forum in relation to different regimes have been outlined. Finally, the possible benefit of the forums' informal powers to recommend has been noted.

Writing reports and presenting evidence
Tribunals

The Tribunals Judiciary have issued a practice direction which sets out the requirements for written reports (Carnwath, 2012). As nurses, you are most likely to be involved in writing social circumstance reports or nursing reports. When reading the requirements, it is important to keep in mind the purpose of the tribunal and the evidence the panel will need to be able to make a sound decision. In answering whether the criteria continue to be met, the panel will be trying to tease out what the effect will be of discharging the patient on both the person's mental health and the risk. It will therefore be important that you reflect on how the powers of the Act are currently being used to promote recovery and manage risk, how necessary they are and what would happen if they were not there. The information required for a nursing report is set out below. For example, when providing information for (a) it will be helpful to know how the patient's current understanding of their treatment compares to that in the past, how it has changed as their treatment has progressed and the implications for the use of the Act. In doing so, it will be important to recognise that treatment is more than just medication.

(iii) In-Patient Nursing Report

11. This report must be up-to-date and specifically prepared for the use of the tribunal. In relation to the patient's current in-patient episode, it must include full details of the following:

(a) the patient's understanding of, and willingness to accept, the current treatment for mental disorder provided or offered;

(b) the level of observation to which the patient is subject;

(c) any occasions on which the patient has been secluded or restrained, including the reasons why seclusion or restraint was considered to be necessary;

(d) any occasions on which the patient has been absent without leave whilst liable to be detained, or occasions when the patient has failed to return when required, after having been granted leave of absence;

(e) any incidents where the patient has harmed themselves or others or threatened such harm, or damaged property or threatened such damage.

When writing the report it will also be important to ensure that you are not breaching your duty of confidentiality to any third party that has provided you with information. If in doubt, you should seek advice from your information governance team. This is particularly important when information has been provided by close family members. Before considering whether to include such information, it will be important that you discuss this with the person, ensure they are aware this means the patient is likely to be informed and seek their view.

Scenario

James is detained under section 3 and has applied for a tribunal. He has been detained for 18 months and has a diagnosis of schizophrenia. When he was admitted, his life was chaotic and he was regularly using a number of different substances. He also did not believe he had a diagnosed mental illness. Since admission he has realised the negative impact that drug use has had on his life and is recognising the need for settled housing and routine occupational activities. He has started a training course at college and is hopeful of employment. Due to his non-compliance with medication, he was started on a depot. This seems to reduce his voices to a level he can manage. However, he often denies he has a mental illness, is reluctant to take the depot and states he only does so because he has to. His history demonstrates that he relapses if he does not receive medical treatment.

Activity 10.1   *Communication*

Consider the information you have on James and write down the parts that are relevant to the information the tribunal needs in relation to point (a) *the patient's understanding of, and willingness to accept, the current treatment for mental disorder provided or offered.*

What extra information may be useful for the tribunal?

There is an outline answer at the end of the chapter.

At the tribunal itself you may be asked to present your report or be asked questions about it. Remember there is an expectation that the parties have read the report. There is therefore no need to verbally present all of it. You may be asked questions by any panel member, the patient or their solicitor. It is important that you answer the questions as calmly and frankly as you can. It may help to use some of these simple techniques. For example, you may want to ensure you give yourself time to think before answering, and so deliberately pause; or if you feel pressured by the style with which a person asks questions, then you can look at them when they ask the question but direct your answer to the judge to begin with and only look back at them when you conclude. This can be particularly useful if you feel you are being interrupted and not given the chance to finish your answer. It is also important to remember that the patient will be present and you will be discussing intimate areas of their life and their liberty. It is therefore important to consider how you can do so respectfully and remember you can point out positives whilst being frank about some of the remaining challenges.

Managers' hearings

The Code of Practice does not give any specific guidance as to the content of nursing reports for managers' hearings, other than stating that a nurse is an example of a key individual who should provide such a report. It will therefore be important for you to familiarise yourself with the standards of your hospital. In the absence of any standard format, you could include the information the tribunal requests. However, it is important to remember that the panel will not contain the same level of expertise that a tribunal does and so will rely more on the assessment of the professionals involved. Consequently, it will be important that you do not take it for granted that specialist terms, phrases or assessments will be understood without an explanation. Being mindful of this is also good practice in ensuring the patient can understand the report.

Section summary

This section has outlined the requirements when writing reports for these decision making forums. We have emphasised the importance of considering what evidence the forum needs when considering decisions in relation to their powers and how asking this question can improve the quality of your report.

Sharing reports with the patient and withholding evidence from the patient

Sharing reports

Except in special circumstances, the patient and their representative should have access to the reports in sufficient time before the hearing or tribunal. For tribunals, the tribunal office will send out the reports to all parties. For managers' hearings, the Code of Practice states that the patient and their representative should be given the reports as soon as they are available and in good time to consider them and point out any inaccuracies. When this is in practice will depend on how much notice has been given about the hearing, how quickly the patient's situation is changing, the complexity of the subject matter and the significance of any contested material. The risk is that any delays in giving the report to the patient could lead to them not being able to properly consider it and take advice. This could lead to unnecessary adjournments or a weakening of the fairness of the hearing. It is therefore important that you recognise the importance of completing reports in a timely fashion and keep those organising the hearing informed.

It is good practice for you to have shared the report with the patient yourself, ideally before submitting it. In doing so, you will need to consider how you can effectively share it with them in a way that enables them to understand it, express their views and consider how they will respond to any issues raised. This can be a difficult process and it is natural to have anxiety about how the patient may react. Some nurses can be concerned that it will affect their therapeutic relationship. However, having difficult conversations is an integral part of meeting the Nursing and Midwifery Council (NMC) Code of Conduct's requirement to *be open and honest, act with integrity and uphold the reputation of your profession* (NMC, 2008). It may also damage your relationship more if the patient is surprised by information you provide during the hearing process or that they are informed by their representative that you are submitting such evidence.

> ### Scenario
>
> *You have written a report about James and want to share it with him. However, you are concerned that it is a lot of information to take in at once and you are unsure how James will react. You arrange a number of one to one meetings with him and agree with him that his independent mental health advocate (IMHA) will also attend. You summarise your report into key issues and information to share in each session and ensure that there is a balance of positives and remaining challenges and concerns. At the meeting the IMHA agrees to take notes and meet with James afterwards to talk about anything he may wish to discuss. In the process you also remind James of his right to legal advice and support.*

Activity 10.2	Communication

Consider a patient with whom you have worked over a period of time. Now imagine that you have to share a report with them. Make a brief list of the following:

- What are their communication needs?
- What could some of the obstacles be to sharing the report?
- What practical steps do you need to take to help them understand and think about the information?
- How would you present the information?

There is an outline answer at the end of the chapter.

Withholding information from the patient

Rule 14 of the Tribunal Rules allows for information to be withheld from the patient. If such information is to be withheld, then the tribunal must be presented with it in a separate document that includes the reason why it should be withheld. The tribunal can only make an order for it to be withheld if they are satisfied that disclosing it would cause serious harm to the patient or another person and that it is proportionate, considering the interests of justice. One of the key interests of justice is ensuring that the patient can fairly engage with the proceedings and present their case. Tribunals do not take these decisions lightly because they consider the patient's liberty to be a very serious issue at stake. It will, therefore, be important not to assume the tribunal will agree to the information being withheld.

If such information is withheld, then it will usually be disclosed to the patient's legal representative, on the undertaking that they do not disclose it to the patient. The patient can then be enabled to present evidence in relation to the general themes within the withheld evidence.

Case study: *RM v. St Andrew's Healthcare* [2010] UKUT 119 (AAC) (23 April 2010)

A patient was detained under section 3 and refused to take medication after being told he had been given it covertly. He had organic delusional disorder, organic personality disorder and epilepsy. He deteriorated and needed more coercive management. He sustained injuries and required restraint and seclusion. He was at increased risk of sudden, unexpected death. He was started on covert medication again. When the issue came once more to the First Tier Tribunal, the hospital requested that this information be withheld from the patient. Although the judge agreed that the risks were serious, he held that there was no way the interests of justice could be served if the information was withheld. When the case was appealed at the Upper Tribunal, the judge agreed, stating: Justice will not be done at the hearing; it will only seem to be done. The real proceedings will have to be conducted out of the patient's sight and knowledge *(para. 27).*

This case study emphasises the high level of significance that the legal system places on the protection of liberty and the fairness of court proceedings. This can often be a shock to practitioners who are trained primarily in promoting positive health and social outcomes and protecting patients' welfare. It also emphasises the importance of seeking proper advice about the implications of not informing detained patients about certain information.

The Code of Practice advises that reports for managers' hearings should be shared with the patient unless panels decide, on recommendations from professionals, that doing so will be likely to cause serious harm to the physical or mental health of the patient or any other individual. It is worth noting that the word 'serious' denotes a level of risk greater than just harm. If you have concerns of this nature, you will need to discuss them with the wider team and be clear what information needs to be withheld and how the criterion of serious harm is met. In line with tribunals, it would also be worth considering how the patient can be supported to respond to the general theme of the concern. In situations such as this it is even more important, in the interest of fairness and equality of power in relationships, that the patient has a legal representative who is aware of the information and can ensure the patient can respond to the general themes.

Section summary

This section has considered how to share your reports effectively with patients and the mechanisms that allow certain information to be withheld from patients in certain circumstances. The patient's right to information in relation to their detention has been emphasised, as has the need not to take withholding evidence lightly and to ensure fairness.

Supporting the patient and the patient's experience of the hearings

As a nurse you are likely to be involved in helping a patient to understand and/or prepare for a tribunal. Patients will come from all different backgrounds and will have differing experiences of formal decision making forums. Some patients may be able to draw on positive experiences from the past or difficult situations they have overcome. These can give a sense of confidence, and practical ways of making the most of the experience or even just getting through it. However, others may never have experienced such forums, have had negative experiences or be anxious because this time it is about them personally. In seeking to support patients, it will therefore be important that you don't make assumptions about their views, expectations, hopes and fears but are prepared to listen to them. If you will also be the one providing evidence, you may want to think about how this could impact upon your ability to support the person and whether another professional, IMHA or other person may be better placed to support the patient through certain aspects of the process.

As already referred to, the CQC and the Administrative Justice and Tribunals Council undertook research to establish patients' views and experiences of the tribunal. The research found that only one in ten patients who responded had help from a nurse and only a minority from advocacy services. The researchers made a number of other recommendations that will be relevant to you. Two key recommendations were that staff members prevent a cycle of delay by ensuring that reports are submitted on time and updates are submitted when necessary. In addition, it was identified that there is a need for greater monitoring of care plans that are aimed at meeting tribunals' conditions for discharge. Finally, the research identified the wider need for staff to ensure all reasonable steps are taken to enable patients to understand their care plans.

Scenario

James and his solicitor approach you before his tribunal and talk about how anxious he is. You are able to support James in planning for the tribunal by talking through a leaflet that explains in what order things will happen and by showing him round the tribunal room. He is anxious about many people talking about his personal details and about not understanding what they are saying. You enable him to talk with his solicitor about this and come up with a plan on how James can ask his solicitor to clarify anything he doesn't understand. Although you are not James's key nurse, you talk to his key nurse and arrange a time for James to go through his key care plans with him.

Activity 10.3   *Reflection*

Consider a patient with whom you have worked who has had a tribunal or who is likely to have one. Make a list of three or four steps you could take to support them through the process. What may you need to research in your own work place to achieve this?

There is an outline answer at the end of the chapter.

Section summary

This section has considered research in relation to patients' experiences of tribunals. You have been asked to begin to think about how you can promote a better experience for patients in your work base.

Chapter summary

In this chapter you have been introduced to routes by which patients can challenge their detention. The make-up of each and the procedures each follow have been outlined. Consideration has also been given to patients' experiences. You should now be in a position to understand your duties in relation to submitting written and oral evidence and should have begun planning how to enable patients to have a better experience of these forums.

Activities: brief outline answers

Activity 10.1

11a of the practice direction requires: *(a) the patient's understanding of, and willingness to accept, the current treatment for mental disorder provided or offered.*

All the information in the scenario will be helpful for the tribunal, as they will need to know about the patient's current views, put this into context in terms of changes in views and draw out the implications in the need for statutory powers to ensure the patient receives treatment. The tribunal would also find it helpful to understand more about: how James's views have changed, what has enabled this and over what time period it has occurred; is this different from the pattern of previous admissions or the same; what level of persuasion James needs to take medication and any common differences between times when he does accept it and does not; and your view as to whether he would object or refuse treatment if not detained and the effectiveness of any contingency plan without statutory powers backing it up.

Activity 10.2

The answers to the questions will very much depend on the circumstances, experience and needs of each individual patient. It is important that you don't make assumptions about patients but consider what their needs are and how best you can support them. Common features, within appropriate answers, may include considering times and places when they will be best disposed to talk about the difficult issues, ensuring you don't use jargon and considering whether an IMHA would help.

Activity 10.3

The answers to this activity will also depend on the specifics of each patient. However, you may want to consider what written information you have about tribunals and managers' hearings and if this is suitable for the patient you had in mind. You may also want to find out more about where the hearings are held in your work place and how the patient is empowered to engage.

Further reading

Care Quality Commission and Administrative Justice and Tribunals Council (2011) *Patients' Experiences of the First-tier Tribunal (Mental Health).* **http://www.cqc.org.uk/sites/default/files/media/documents/ajtc_cqc_first_tier_tribunal_report_final.pdf**

The research into patients' experiences of tribunals is worth reading in full.

Department of Health (2008) *Reference Guide to the Mental Health Act 1983.* London: TSO.

Department of Health (2008) *Code of Practice: Mental Health Act 1983.* London: TSO.

Detailed discussion of tribunals' and managers' hearings' powers, procedures and application and reference rights.

Useful websites

http://www.justice.gov.uk/tribunals/mental-health

Information about mental health tribunals.

Multiple choice questions

1. A section 2 patient can apply for a tribunal

   (a)   As many times as they like
   (b)   Never as they must wait to be put on section 3

(c)   Once, at any time

(d)   Once, within the first 14 days

2. A section 3 patient can apply to a managers' hearing

    (a)   As many times as they like

    (b)   Once in each renewal period

    (c)   Never, tribunals are for section 3 patients

    (d)   Twice in each period of renewal

3. A tribunal must discharge a section 3 patient

    (a)   Only if their doctor or another doctor agrees

    (b)   If the statutory criteria are not met

    (c)   Only if the tribunal are satisfied they will not relapse at any time in the future

    (d)   Only if the patient proves they are fit for discharge

4. The tribunal medical member

    (a)   Provides evidence to the tribunal but does not make a decision

    (b)   Provides evidence based on their interview of the patient and makes a decision about the statutory criteria

    (c)   Can discharge the patient if they disagree with the patient's consultant

    (d)   Only interviews the patient if the consultant asks for a second opinion

Glossary

assault   Any act which intentionally – or possibly recklessly – causes another person to apprehend immediate and unlawful personal violence

AWOL   Absent without leave

community patients   Those treated outside hospital or other institutional settings. In the context of community treatment orders the term has a specific meaning. That is, a person under a community treatment order

community treatment order   A statutory regime on which patients who have been detained on longer term sections for treatment may be discharged. It has conditions attached and the patient may be recalled to hospital in certain circumstances

informal patients   Those treated in hospital who are not detained but have not been able to consent to the admission because they lack capacity to do so. However, the term is commonly used to refer to all patients that are not detained

Mental Health Act administrator   An administrator normally responsible for the management of paperwork and processes related to the Mental Health Act. This includes the scrutiny of detention papers

qualifying patients   Those eligible to receive the services of specialist independent mental health advocates. Section 130C of the Mental Health Act sets out who is eligible to receive support from an independent mental health advocate. This includes those who are either detained in hospital (including those who are on authorised leave), subject to guardianship or on supervised community treatment. People detained in hospital under either emergency or holding powers are not eligible. All patients who are considering treatment under section 57 and anyone under 18 who is being considered for electro-convulsive therapy are also eligible. It is a legal requirement to tell people who are eligible to receive a service from an independent mental health advocate about their right to receive it

recall to hospital   The power to compel a patient under a community treatment order to return to hospital, if necessary against their will

regulatory authority   The national authority with statutory responsibility to regulate and monitor certain aspects of the Mental Health Act

section 17 leave   Patients detained under the Mental Health Act can only normally leave hospital if their absence is authorised by their responsible clinician. This is often referred to as section 17 leave

second opinion appointed doctor   A doctor appointed by the Care Quality Commission to consider approving certain treatment plans of detained patients. They have the power not to approve the treatment plans

statutory consultee   A person whom a second opinion appointed doctor consults as part of their assessment process

supervised community treatment   The term used by the Code of Practice to describe all aspects of the community treatment order regime

vicariously liable   This legal term means that in circumstances in which the first person is in a special relationship with a second person, the first person can be held responsible for any harm the second person causes. For example, a local authority is responsible for the actions of its employees when they are undertaking their employment duties

voluntary patient   One who has consented to be treated in hospital

Answers to multiple choice questions

Chapter 1

1. (c) 2007
2. (c) Parliament
3. (c) 1930
4. (a) *Reference Guide to the Mental Health Act 1983*

Chapter 2

1. (a) Everyone in the UK
2. (b) Financial means
3. (d) That they cannot make a complaint
4. (c) Patients may not be deprived of their liberty

Chapter 3

1. (c) Health care assistant or domestic worker
2. (c) Brother or sister
3. (a) Appoint doctors for the purpose of carrying out a second opinion under the Act (SOAD)
4. (a) Responsible clinician

Chapter 4

1. (d) Is an informal patient who can give valid consent to be admitted and is agreeable to receiving care and treatment
2. (d) Any disorder or disability of the mind
3. (d) May last for up to 28 days. The patient may appeal within the first 14 days of the detention
4. (d) Can be applied by a nurse of the prescribed class, is not renewable and the patient must be already receiving treatment in hospital for a mental disorder

Chapter 5

1. (b) The Care Quality Commission
2. (c) A patient on community treatment order recalled to hospital
3. (a) From when the medicine was first administered under that period of detention
4. (d) In an emergency

Chapter 6

1. (b) Their responsible clinician
2. (d) Necessary in the interests of the patient or the protection of others
3. (d) A responsible clinician must consider a community treatment order if a patient has been on section 17 leave for longer than seven days
4. (b) Withhold the leave on medical grounds

Chapter 7

1. (c) A patient detained under section 3
2. (c) The responsible clinician can recall them to hospital if they are in need of further treatment as a recalled patient due to risk to self or others
3. (c) 72 hours
4. (d) They cannot be subject to section 5 holding powers

Chapter 8

1. (a) 72 hours
2. (c) Section 47
3. (c) Never
4. (b) Restrictions should be based on individual risk assessments and not blanket bans

Chapter 9

1. (a) Public law, tort law, contract of employment, statute
2. (a) They are protected from liability unless the act was done in bad faith or without reasonable care
3. (b) Potentially a safeguarding issue
4. (b) The act must be a criminal offence

Chapter 10

1. (d) Once, within the first 14 days
2. (a) As many times as they like
3. (b) If the statutory criteria are not met
4. (b) Provides evidence based on their interview with the patient and makes a decision about the statutory criteria

Bibliography

Bach S and Ellis P (2011) *Leadership, Management and Team Working in Nursing*. Exeter: Learning Matters.

Barber, P, Brown, RE and Martin, D (2012) *Mental Health Law in England and Wales: A guide for mental health professionals*, 2nd edition. London: Sage/Learning Matters.

Bowen, P (2007) *Blackstone's Guide to the Mental Health Act 2007*. Oxford: Oxford University Press.

Bradley, Lord K (2009) *The Bradley Report: Lord Bradley's review of people with mental health problems or learning disabilities in the criminal justice system*. London: Department of Health.

Burns, T et al. (2013) *Community Treatment Orders for Patients with Psychosis (Octet): A randomised controlled trial*. http://www.thelancet.com/journals/lancet/article/PIIS0140-6736%2813%2960107-5/fulltext.

Churchill, R (2008) *International Experiences of Using Community Treatment Orders*. London: Department of Health.

Care Quality Commission (CQC) (2010a) *Monitoring the Use of the Mental Health Act in 2009/10*. http://www.cqc.org.uk/sites/default/files/media/documents/cqc_monitoring_the_use_of_the_mental_health_act_in_200910_main_report_tagged.pdf.

Care Quality Commission (CQC) (March 2010b) *Leave of Absence under the Mental Health Act*. Newcastle: Care Quality Commission.

Care Quality Commission (CQC) (2011) *Monitoring the Mental Health Act 2010/11*. Newcastle: Care Quality Commission.

Care Quality Commission (CQC) (2012) *Monitoring the Mental Health Act Annual Report 2010/11*. Newcastle: Care Quality Commission.

Care Quality Commission (CQC) (2013) *Monitoring the Mental Health Act 2011/12*. Newcastle: Care Quality Commission.

Care Quality Commission and Administrative Justice and Tribunals Council (2011) *Patients' Experiences of the First-tier Tribunal (Mental Health)*. Newcastle: Care Quality Commission and London: Administrative Justice and Tribunals Council.

Care Quality Commission and National Mental Health Development Unit (April 2011) 'Count me in 2010'. Newcastle: Care Quality Commission.

Dawson, J et al. (2003) Ambivalence about community treatment orders. *International Journal of Law and Psychiatry*, 6: 243–255.

Department of Health (2000) *No Secrets: Guidance on developing and implementing multi-agency policies and procedures to protect vulnerable adults from abuse*. London: Department of Health.

Department of Health (2007) *Human Rights in Healthcare: A framework for local action.* London: Department of Health.

Department of Health (2008a) *Reference Guide to the Mental Health Act 1983.* London: TSO.

Department of Health (2008b) *Code of Practice: Mental Health Act 1983.* London: TSO.

Department of Health (2010a) *NHS Constitution for England.* London: Department of Health.

Department of Health (2010b) *Race Equality Action Plan: A five year review.* London: Department of Health.

Department of Health (2011) *Good Practice Procedure Guide: The transfer and remission of adult prisoners under s47 and s48 of the Mental Health Act.* London: Department of Health.

Fennell, P (2007) *Mental Health: The new law.* Wiltshire: Jordan.

Francis, R (2010) *Independent Inquiry into Care Provided by Mid Staffordshire NHS Foundation Trust January 2005–March 2009.* London: TSO.

Gilbert, C and Plant, N (2010) Supervised community treatment brings changes to the nurse's role. *Mental Health Practice,* 13(6): 31–34.

Griffith, R and Tengnah, C (2010) *Law and Professional Issues in Nursing.* Exeter: Learning Matters.

HIW (2011) *Monitoring the Use of the Mental Health Act in 2009–2010.* Caerphilly: Health Inspectorate for Wales.

Jones, R (2010) *The Mental Health Act Manual,* 13th edition. London: Thomson Reuters (Legal Ltd).

Mental Health Act Commission (2001) *Ninth Biannual Report.* Nottingham: Mental Health Act Commission.

Nursing and Midwifery Council (NMC) (2008) *The Code: Standards of conduct, performance and ethics for nurses and midwives.* London: NMC

Nursing and Midwifery Council (NMC) (September 2010) *Standards for Pre-registration Nursing Education.* http://standards.nmc-uk.org.

Pereira, S and Clinton, C (2002) *Mental Health Policy Implementation Guide: National minimum standards for general adult services in psychiatric intensive care units (PICU) and low secure environments.* London: Department of Health.

Singleton, N et al. (2001) Psychiatric morbidity among adults living in private households, 2000. London: Office for National Statistics.

Smith, S (2010) *Supervised Community Treatment: Briefing paper 2.* Manchester: Mental Health Alliance.

Primary legislation

Criminal Justice Act 2003

Employment Rights Act 1996

Human Rights Act 1998

Mental Capacity Act 2005

Mental Health Act 1959

Mental Health Act 1983

Mental Health (Amendment) Act 2007

National Assistance Act 1948

Tribunals Courts and Enforcement Act 2007

Cases

AH v. *West London MHT* [2011] UKUT 74 (AAC)

CNWL NHS Foundation Trust v. *H-JH* [2012] UKUT 210 (AAC)

G v. *Central and North West London Mental Health NHS Trust* [2007] ALL ER (D) (286)

Herczegfalvy v. *Austria* [1993] 15 EHRR 437

HL v. *UK* [2004] ECHR 471

J Council v. *GU & Ors* [2012] EWHC 3531 (COP)

Kay v. *United Kingdom* [1998] 17821/91 (1993) ECHR 61

Munjaz v. *UK* 2913/06 (2012) MHLO 79 (ECHR)

R. (on the application of DR) v. *Mersey Care NHS Trust* [2002] EWHC 1810 (Admin)

R. (on the application of CS) v. *Mental health Review Tribunal* [2004] EWHC 2958 (Admin)

Rabone v. *Pennine Care NHS Foundation Trust* [2012] UKSC 2 (2012) MHLO 6

R(H) v. *MHRT North and East London* Region [2001] EWCA Civ 415

R (M) v. *Secretary of State for Health* [2003] EWHC 1094 (Admin).

RM v. *St Andrew's Healthcare* [2010] UKUT 119 (AAC) (23 April 2010)

Savage v. *South Essex Partnership NHS Foundation Trust* [2008] UKHL 74

TTM v. *LB Hackney* [2011] EWCA Civ 4

Practice directions

Carnwath, R (Lord Justice) (2012) *Practice Direction First-tier Tribunal Health Education and Social Care Chamber Statements and reports in mental health cases*, Tribunals Judiciary, 6 April. http://www.judiciary.gov.uk/Resources/JCO/Documents/Practice%20Directions/Tribunals/hesc-statements-in-mh-cases-062012.pdf

Index